Systemic Violence of the Law

Global Critical Caribbean Thought

Series Editors: Lewis R. Gordon, Professor of Philosophy, UCONN-Storrs, and Honorary Professor, Rhodes University, South Africa; Jane Anna Gordon, Associate Professor of Political Science, UCONN-Storrs; and Nelson Maldonado-Torres, Associate Professor of Latino and Caribbean Studies, Rutgers, School of Arts and Sciences

This series, published in partnership with the Caribbean Philosophical Association, turns the lens on the unfolding nature and potential future shape of the globe by taking concepts and ideas that while originating out of very specific contexts share features that lend them transnational utility. Works in the series engage with figures including Frantz Fanon, CLR James, Paulo Freire, Aime Cesaire, Edouard Glissant and Walter Rodney, and concepts such as coloniality, creolization, decoloniality, double consciousness and la facultdad.

Titles in the Series
Race, Rights and Rebels: Alternatives to Human Rights and Development from the Global South
Julia Suárez Krabbe
Decolonizing Democracy: Power in a Solid State
Ricardo Sanin-Restrepo
Geopolitics and Decolonization: Perspectives from the Global South
Edited by Lewis R. Gordon and Fernanda Bragato
The Existence of the Mixed Race Damnés: Decolonialism, Class, Gender, Race
Daphne V. Taylor-Garcia
The Desiring Modes of Being Black: Literature and Critical Theory
Jean-Paul Rocchi
Decrypting Power
Edited by Ricardo Sanín-Restrepo
Looking Through Philosophy in Black: Memoirs
Mabogo Percy More
Black Existentialism: Essays on the Transformative Thought of Lewis R. Gordon
Edited by danielle davis
A Decolonial Philosophy of Indigenous Colombia: Time, Beauty, and Spirit in Kamëntsá Culture
By Juan Alejandro Chindoy Chindoy
Blackening Britain: Caribbean Radicalism from Windrush to Decolonization
By James G. Cantres
Systemic Violence of the Law: Colonialism and International Investment
Enrique Prieto-Rios

Systemic Violence of the Law

Colonialism and International Investment

Enrique Prieto-Rios

Faculty of Law, Universidad del Rosario

ROWMAN & LITTLEFIELD
Lanham • Boulder • New York • London

Published by Rowman & Littlefield
An imprint of The Rowman & Littlefield Publishing Group, Inc.
4501 Forbes Boulevard, Suite 200, Lanham, Maryland 20706
www.rowman.com

6 Tinworth Street, London SE11 5AL, United Kingdom

Copyright © 2021 by Enrique Prieto-Rios

All rights reserved. No part of this book may be reproduced in any form or by any electronic or mechanical means, including information storage and retrieval systems, without written permission from the publisher, except by a reviewer who may quote passages in a review.

British Library Cataloguing in Publication Information Available

Library of Congress Cataloging-in-Publication Data

Names: Prieto-Rios, Enrique, author.
Title: Systemic violence of the law : colonialism and international investment / Enrique Prieto-Rios.
Description: Lanham, Maryland : Rowman & Littlefield, [2021] | Series: Global critical Caribbean thought | Based on author's thesis (doctoral - University of London, 2017) issued under title: Thinking on international investment law : from colonialism to international systemic violence. | Includes bibliographical references and index.
Identifiers: LCCN 2021015901 (print) | LCCN 2021015902 (ebook) | ISBN 9781538157848 (cloth) | ISBN 9781538157855 (epub) ISBN 9781538157862 (pbk)
Subjects: LCSH: Investments, Foreign (International law) | Law and economic development. | Developing countries—International status. | Colonialism—Economic aspects. | Imperialism—Economic aspects.
Classification: LCC K3830 .P744 2021 (print) | LCC K3830 (ebook) | DDC 346/.092—dc23
LC record available at https://lccn.loc.gov/2021015901
LC ebook record available at https://lccn.loc.gov/2021015902

To Diana and Tomás

Contents

Acknowledgements	ix
Introduction	1
1　Systemic Violence and International Investment Law	15
2　Fault-Lines: In-between Moving Abroad and Attracting Foreign Direct Investment	35
3　The Riddle of Treaties and Awards	51
4　The Encrypted Discourse of International Investment Law: Hierarchy, Knowledge and Power	65
5　Neoliberal Ideology: A Tale of Persistence and Hegemony	83
6　IIL: An Autopoietic System	99
Conclusion	115
Bibliography	129
Index	149
About the Author	155

Acknowledgements

Despite the loneliness and individual endeavour that is implied in the writing of a book, to have reached this point of having a definitive version of the text would had been impossible without the support of institutions, family and friends. Above all, I would like to express significant debt and my greatest gratitude to Professor Lewis Gordon for believing in my work and encouraging me to pursue this project; he raised me up when circumstances seemed uncertain and my strength to continue was fading. Without his mentorship, support and patience this book would never have seen the light of day.

I also would like to thank Professor Oscar Guardiola-Rivera for developing my interests on the relationship between International Investment Law and the colonial past. He also brought new intellectual challenges to the table. Oscar is not only a great thinker, and a fantastic and dedicated supervisor, but he is also an inspiring person who taught me the value of perseverance.

I would also like to express my everlasting gratitude to Prof. Luis Eslava, to Juan Pablo Pontón Serra and Robert Joseph Blaise MacLean for their honest and constructive feedback that helped me immensely in better structuring the arguments presented in this book. Along the same lines, I am grateful for all the comments and feedback received on my research during the writing workshop at the Institute of Global Law and Policy – IGLP, the annual conferences at the Caribbean Philosophical Association – CPA, my time as a visiting fellow at the Globe Institute at Warwick University working with profs. Celine Tan and Illan Wall and at Osgoode Hall Law School at York University working with prof. Gus Van Harten. Also, all the feedback received during the academic conferences that I attended during my PhD studies. I am also grateful with the International Economic Law Collective an epistemic community that has helped me not to feel alone while pursuing alternative research on International Investment Law.

Furthermore, I extend my gratitude to the Birkbeck intellectual community, especially all those who offered me their friendship, constant feedback and emotional support, in helping me complete this research. Chiefly, I would like to thank Paddy McDaid, Mayur Suresh, Kanika Sharma, Anastasia Tataryn, Carolina Olarte Olarte, Tshepo Madlingozi, Kojo Koram and Tara Mulqueen.

Others to whom I owe a lot for making the cold days warm, and who were essential in the completion of this research are Juan Díaz, Camila Bernal, Rodrigo Paris, Paola Forero, Camilo Garavito, Juan José and Mauricio Roesel, Jenny Ruiz-Wilkey, Luke Wilkey and Ivan Pulido. Your unconditional friendship was an essential emotional pillar during my time in London; all of you became my second family in a foreign land.

I also want to express my gratitude to friends and colleagues who helped me immensely on my return to Colombia and who opened doors for me to continue my academic life in Bogotá. To the Faculty of Law at the Universidad del Rosario which opened its doors to me to join such a vibrant academic community. To Juan Carlos Forero Ramirez, Lina M. Céspedes-Baez and Jose Manuel Restrepo Abondano who believed in me and gave me the opportunity to begin my academic career at the Universidad del Rosario. To Alejandro Cheyne, Jose Alberto Gaitán and Laura Victoria Garcia Matamoros who offered me all the necessary support to complete this book. To my colleagues in the Research Group on International Law who have also supported me during this journey. Finally, to my team at the Research Direction who were patient and were comprehending of the time requirements for the writing of an academic book. I also would like to thank the School Law at the Universidad de los Andes especially to René Urueña and Helena Alviar Garcia, thanks to whom I returned to Colombia and who believe in my research and in me.

Last but not least, I want to thank my family, especially my mother and father who were always supportive and who never gave up on me despite the time and the emotional crises linked to this type of work. My father hoped to see this book become a reality, unfortunately, he passed away before witnessing its completion. Wherever he is I am sure he will celebrate its publication. I also want to thank Tomas my new-born baby who has been patient while watching his father toil away. Finally, I want to thank Diana, my wife, to whom this achievement equally belongs. I am extremely grateful for her decision to join me on this journey, for her sleepless nights helping me with book 'stuff', for all her emotional support in all those challenging times when I was not sure about moving forward, for her patience, for reading all my chapters more than a hundred times, but most importantly for never ceasing to believe in me.

Introduction

When plunder becomes a way of life for a group of men in a society, over the course of time they create for themselves a legal system that authorizes it and a moral code that glorifies it. (Frédéric Bastiat)

IIL SYSTEM IN CONTEXT

In this book, I want to share an alternative narrative regarding the International Investment Law system (IIL). In doing so, I wish to begin by historically contextualising IIL so as to present events that led to its worldwide consolidation. By the nineteenth century, processes of colonisation took Western European powers to all regions of the world (Rist 2008). In economic terms, colonialism was characterised by the plunder of resources and the expropriation of the surplus from the colonised (Bulhan 1985). It is important to recall that the origins of capitalism and colonialism are intertwined, as endless accumulation was only possible thanks to the high influx of resources from colonies to the centre (specifically coming from the Americas) (Dussel 2014, 69).

The change from feudalism to capitalism was possible thanks to the labour, gold and silver flowing from the Americas that permitted high returns and allowed to the West high levels of accumulation of capital (Frank 2009, 282) (Guardiola-Rivera 2010, 78–84). These actions allowed the colonial metropolis to accumulate both its own surplus and the colonies' surplus. This increased, thereby, the ability of the metropolis to produce more goods, thus moving to the top position in the global production chain while creating the rules to regulate global markets to maintain their economic advantage.

As stated by Fanon: 'The colonial system, in fact, was only interested in certain riches, certain natural resources, to be exact those that fuelled its industries' (Fanon 2004, 56). A clear example of these dynamics was the restriction imposed by Britain upon India in textile production (Guardiola-Rivera, 2013, p. 69). The specialisation enhanced the differentiation between the metropolis and the periphery. The periphery was forced to specialise in raw materials, whereas the centre focused on the production of manufactured products which have a higher return (Guardiola-Rivera, 2013, p. 67).

The colonial period was the perfect time to foster the movement and settlement of capitalists into the periphery, seeking new business opportunities in the colonised lands. Although the investment opportunities during colonial times involved the risk of not making any gain and losing the investment, as happened with the Scottish voyage to the Americas,[1] there was also a level of certainty offered by military superiority as well as the economic, legal and political control exercised by the colonial power upon the colonies (Guardiola-Rivera, 2010). The colonial structure clearly granted metropolis countries, such as Spain, the United Kingdom and/or France, a structural advantage to move forward in the global market.

The combination of colonial practices with the expansion of capitalism, created an uneven international economic structure in which a few societies exploited and plundered peripheral societies (under colonial or imperial control) expropriating its surplus and transferring it from the periphery to the centre.[2] One part of the globe was deemed to provide raw materials and cheap labour while the other, the winners, were deemed to enjoy the benefits of those raw materials brought from the periphery,[3] to produce manufactured goods and to enjoy its profitability. Such an uneven economic structure was

---

[1] William Paterson, a Scottish adventurer, led a voyage to the Americas. In 1695, the Scottish Parliament enacted the Act stabilising the Darien Company of Scotland granting the power to trade with Africa and the Indies. This Act was opposed by William III as response to the lobbying pressure of the East Indian Company. Scottish received England's rejection as direct insult. Hence, money from private Scottish hands came to support the enterprise. On 26 July 1698, the voyage to the Americas began with 1,200 men and women on the Ships Unicorn, St Andrew, Caledonia, Endeavour and Dolphin. The vessels reached the coast of the Panamanian isthmus by 3 November 1968. The voyage went totally wrong as result of malaria, yellow fever, the ban imposed by the English Crown to trade with the Scotts, and the several Spanish attempts to attack the Scottish settlement. On 20 June 1969, the Scotts left the isthmus only 360 crew members survived and the money collected was totally lost. (Guardiola-Rivera, What if Latin America Rule the World? How the South Will Take the North into the Twenty-Second Century, 2010).

[2] Marx talks about two types of surplus, that is, relative and absolute. Absolute refers to the increase of labour to produce commodities for sale. Relative surplus includes the improvement on the organisation of the workplace, technology, or any other form that does not require hiring more labour or paying more. In both cases, the capitalist or the firm compete against each other to accumulate more profit. See: Karl Marx, *Capital: A Critique of Political Economy* (Volume I, Progress Publishers, 2016), 358–75, <https://www.marxists.org/archive/marx/works/download/pdf/Capital-Volume-I.pdf> accessed 6 November 2020.

[3] The concept of centre and periphery was coined by Raul Prebisch.

deepened with the industrial revolution, as it broadened the economic gap between the centre and the periphery, allowing European capitalists, entrepreneurs and the economy of central countries to create new forms of profit (this global division also contributed in the commodity fetishism).[4]

The economic power, combined with narratives of social and cultural superiority, granted the West the monopoly to construct the discourse of different disciplines such as law (including of course international law and IIL), economics and politics, among others, and the legitimacy to transplant and to impose them upon the periphery (Anghie 2007). For instance, 'the East Indian Company' was an investor for trade which developed political aspirations to protect its economic interests, and eventually colonised the country' (Perry-Kessaris 2008, 64).

In the traditional narrative on IIL, the role played by the colonial structure tends to be forgotten. Rather, the antecedents of the IIL are usually traced back to the sixteenth century when European countries began signing commercial treaties aimed at facilitating trade between nations guaranteeing the freedom of commerce and equality of treatment between two nations and promoting the settlement of foreigners in different jurisdictions for commercial purposes (Connell 1961).

According to this traditional narrative, with the increase of global trade, by the end of the eighteenth century, Western European countries as well as North America began signing Friendship Commerce and Navigation agreements (FCN). These treaties aimed at promoting trade between nations and at addressing certain aspects related to the treatment of foreigners and their property in other jurisdictions. FCNs were only possible between sovereign countries. In the case of colonies, FCN treaties were not necessary as the territories were an extension of the metropolis. Colonies depended economically, legally and politically on the centre and did not enjoy the right of full sovereignty and autonomy. However, once countries reached independence, as in the case of Latin America, Western countries pursued the negotiation of FCNs. Foreign-owned property settled in a different jurisdiction was expected to be treated in accordance with customary international law, imposing the duty on host states to treat foreigners and their property following some international minimum standards (Vandevelde 2005). Among those minimum requirements was that expropriation required appropriate compensation (Christie 1962).

Newly sovereign states were invited to join the global community as independent and sovereign states on the grounds of entering to an already constructed international system that already had its rules in place (public international law). For the newly independent countries, sovereignty

---

[4] Commodity fetishism understood as the action when production as a relationship between commodities and money in the context of a market.

appeared as a principle barring other countries from interfering in the internal affairs of another country. However, as a result of the colonial and imperial constructed international structure, sovereignty in the periphery did not mean total autonomy (Wallerstein, Historical Capitalism with Capitalist Civilisation 2011). Newly independent states, although sovereign, were not equal in economic and geopolitical terms (Anghie 2007).

MOVING FORWARD

Traditional narrative on IIL, hides the fact that contemporary IIL appeared in the international arena as a response to the decolonisation processes of the second half of the twentieth century. IIL became an instrument to maintain certain levels of legal, political and economic control over former colonies and other territories that were previously; under imperial rule. IIL was presented as a technocratic, objective and depoliticised solution for the treatment of foreign investors abroad (Rogers 2014).

IIL begins its period of consolidation with the first Bilateral Investment Treaty (BIT) between Germany and the Islamic Republic of Pakistan in 1959 followed by other Western European countries signing other BITs. This first BIT started a new "innovative" period of post-colonial bilateralism to protect economic interests of capital exporting countries in the newly decolonised territories. France concluded its first BIT in 1960, the Netherlands in 1963, Sweden in 1971 and among others the United Kingdom in 1981 (Salacuse and Sullivan 2009). The total number of treaties signed between 1959 and 1969 was seventy-five (Vandevelde 2005). The United States began a process in 1981 moving from NFC to the creation of its own BIT programme under the presidency of Ronald Reagan; it joined the 'BITs club', signing twenty-four BITs between 1982 and 2011 (Dolzer y Stewvens 1995).

The process of expansion of the IIL system also included efforts to set up a global multilateral agreement for the protection of foreign investors, even though the trend of signing bilateral treaties for the protection of foreign investments was continuing. In this way, in 1961, the OECD made public the Draft Convention on the International Responsibility of States for Injuries to Aliens, and in 1967, published the Draft Convention on the Protection of Foreign Property, neither of which gained sufficient support world-wide to become a multi-lateral binding treaty (Miles, The Origins of International Investment Law: Empire, Environment and The Safeguard of Capital 2013).

Likewise, Aron Broches, who was the General Counsel of the World Bank for twenty years until 1979 (Newyork Times 1997), proposed the creation of a framework for the settlement of investment disputes in order to depoliticise the resolution of conflicts between host states and foreign investors (Miles,

The Origins of International Investment Law: Empire, Environment and The Safeguard of Capital 2013). Aron's proposal culminated in the creation of the International Centre for Settlement of Investment Disputes (ICSID) in 1966 which transformed into an essential institution for the functioning of the IIL system.

The neoliberal ideological shift of 1970s, ignited by the economic conditions of the time, also played in favour of strengthening the IIL system world-wide. Developing countries shifted their priorities from defending their sovereign rights and independently ruling their internal affairs, to joining the global market and to creating a political and legal environment appropriate to attracting foreign investment. Such investment was considered an essential step on the path to reach the promised land of development.

Proliferation of BITs did not occur until the 1990s, when there was a shortage of international credit forcing capital-importing states to rely on foreign aid and foreign investments to pursue programmes of infrastructure, among others (Kaushal 2009). Another factor for the proliferation of BITs was the influence of the World Bank and the International Monetary Fund (IMF) in developing countries. The IIL system was portrayed as the most suitable of instruments to attract foreign investment, which, according to them, was essential for development.

Linking foreign investment to development kicked off a race to the bottom among developing countries to attract foreign investment, entering into more BITs and FTAs and adopting regulations favourable to Multinational Corporations (MNCs) in order to become more attractive to foreign investors (Rist 2008). This competition simultaneously deepened the divisions among developing countries,[5] resembling the old colonial practice of dividing colonised continents for the benefit of the colonisers (F. Fanon 2004).

The international web of International Investment Agreements (IIA) has continued a process of expansion; in 2019, the number of IIA's signed reached a total of 3,284.[6] The figures show that Western countries and MNCs have focused on the construction of an international regime of treaties to offer an enhanced protection to foreign investor´s economic interests above the interests of the communities. The globalisation process of the twentieth century has been accompanied by an agenda to incorporate developing countries into the global economy (Faundez and Tan 2010).

---

[5] One example is the case of the FTA negotiated between Peru, Colombia and the European Union. Colombia and Peru decided to apart themselves from the other countries aiming at winning the race of investment attraction.
[6] UNCTAD, 'World Investment Report: International Production Beyond the Pandemic' (2020) United Nations <https://unctad.org/es/system/files/official-document/wir2020_en.pdf > accessed 20 November 2020.

A SYSTEM TO RESOLVE CONFLICTS?

The IIL system and specifically its Investment State Dispute Settlement (ISDS) procedure has been hailed as an important advancement in the protection of foreign investor´s rights and in the peaceful settlement of disputes. It is argued that ISDS offers the benefit that conflicts are resolved by individuals with relevant expertise and in a quicker way than domestic courts. Within this context of investment arbitration, arbitrators are perceived as the defenders of international law that in general is portrayed as the law of freedom, equality and neutrality. However, behind the existence and operation of the system, there is a distrust of the judicial operators in developing countries. In this regard, Anthea Roberts states the following:

> Comprehending the investment treaty system has proven just as problematic. Investment treaties are clearly creatures of public international law: they are entered into by two or more states and are substantively governed by public international law. However, they are distinct from most public international law treaties because the vast majority of them permit investors to bring arbitral claims directly against host states based on procedural rules and enforcement mechanisms developed largely in the context of international commercial arbitration and investor-state contracts. Accordingly, the system grafts private international law dispute resolution mechanisms on to public international law treaties. (Roberts 2013)

In this way, the existence of an international system for the protection of foreign assets, as an alternative to domestic courts, resembles the colonial past when foreigners from Western colonial powers enjoyed special legal treatment in the colonies as well as in other independent countries subjugated by the West. As happened during colonial times, today's alternative arbitral investment tribunals are linked to concepts of Western epistemological superiority and distrust of the Orient (Said 2007).

On the one hand, offering such certainty to the economic future of the investor, combined with the reduction of barriers as well as existence of the necessary technological financial platforms allows capital to flow more swiftly within the global market (Dussel, 16 Tesis de Economía Política: Interpretación Filosófica 2014). On the other hand, the enhanced protection offered to the foreign investor guarantees that whenever there is a legal or illegal interference with the investor's economic interests, there must be compensation even, if the measure adopted has been adopted to comply with other obligations of international law or to protect higher interests such as the environment. However, such an enhanced protection based upon neoliberal principles clashes with notions of the rule of law, human rights, people's rights and environmental rights, among others (M. Sornarajah 2017).

Academics, practitioners, civil society, international organisations and policy makers have raised constant criticism against the negative consequences of the IIL system (Schill, International Investment Law and Comparative Public Law an Introduction 2010). Most of the criticisms point to the limitations imposed upon host countries to regulate in respect to aspects of social interest, affecting the weakest members of the host society, and for maintaining an unequal global distribution, thus preventing the host economy from climbing up the economic ladder (Ho 2007).

Also, the enhanced protection offered to foreign investors by the IIL system, and specifically the possibility of taking their claim before an investment tribunal challenging sovereign decisions, without exhausting local remedies imposes a real threat to the regulatory activity of the host state (a requirement in other regimes such as Human Rights) (Harten, A Case for an International Investment Court 2008). As stated by, Anthea Roberts:

> Investors are increasingly challenging specific regulatory actions (such as the denial of building or operating permits) or general regulatory measures (such as legislation concerning the economy, environment, human rights, or health and safety) that adversely affect them. Instead of being contractual disputes between private parties, these disputes concern public actions and involve public interests. Accordingly, investment arbitrations permit challenges to governmental conduct in a manner reminiscent of judicial review under domestic public law. (Roberts 2013)

IIL, and the ISDS as its most important conflict resolution mechanism, complies with an end of keeping the government on track albeit in facing economic sanctions in the form of compensations.

The IIL system is also affecting Western developed countries as the system is entering into unchartered waters. MNCs have adopted a transnational and an anonymous character, fading away the classic division of centre and periphery as the geographical links are not evident any more (Castro-Gómez, Guardiola-Rivera and Benavides 1999).

The foregoing does not hide that there has been, and is, a constant global structural injustice that affects both the worst and the weakest in the Global South promoting forms of exploitation (Baxi 2009). Hence, considering the global socio-economic situation whereby existing differences between developed and developing countries, developing countries continue being the most affected by the limitations imposed by the IIL system.

ABOUT THIS WORK

Although plenty of ink has been spent on studying IIL, it being an overworked field of research, I want to offer in this book an alternative narrative to the analysis of the IIL system contributing in innovative manner to the ongoing discussions. In doing so this book takes a non-normative, non-conclusive, non-disciplinary approach to the topic pursuing an inwardly critical inquiry. It problematises the production of "truths" surrounding the IIL system and how it affects the present condition of the IIL system as something contingent and not given (Koopman 2013). In this context, I argue that IIL system is an instrument that facilitates systemic violence thanks to its network of treaties and arbitral tribunals as well as the vectors of encryption, its neoliberal ideology and its autopoietic process to face changes and criticisms.

This book is the result of my pressing need to contest and challenge the IIL system from my standpoint of a Third World Academic, analysing and creating awareness about the imbalances of the system and the facilitation of situations of systemic violence. In pursuing this work, I have proceeded as a bricoleur and as a collector,[7] freely drawing from a variety of disciplines and thinkers whose works are apparently not consistent with one another (Bryant 2011, 27). Bricoleur and collector, also in the sense I had to negotiate my intellectual resources using several theoretical standpoints, using approaches from different theorists and from different disciplines, including the transferring of concepts among disciplines (Gordon, Africana Thought and African-Diasporic Studies 2006, 592) (Rottleuthner 1988).

In this work, I moved from the traditional standing point of analysis of the IIL system that tents to be epistemic and disciplinary closed, limiting the discussion to the discipline of Public International Law. In doing so I am also expressing a criticism and frustration of academic works in this field. In this regard, Lewis Gordon states the following:

> Disciplinary decadence, as we have seen, is the process of critical decay within a field or discipline. In such instance, the proponent ontologizes his or her discipline far beyond its scope. Thus, a decadent scientist criticizes the humanities for not being scientific; a decadent literary scholar criticizes scientists and social scientists for not being literary or intellectual; a decadent social scientist sins in two directions – by criticizing either the humanities for not being social scientific or social sciences for not being scientific in accord with, say, physics or biology. And, of course, the decadent historian criticizes all for not being philosophical. The public dimension of evidence is here subordinated by the

---

[7] Bricoleur: from French – a person who constructs bricoleges is somebody who creates using whatever materials are available.

discipline or field's functioning, literally, as the world. Thus, although another discipline or field may offer evidence to the contrary, it could, literally, be ignored simply on the basis of not being the point of view of one's discipline or field. (L. Gordon 2015)

I am fully aware that this book could be disregarded by insiders as nonsense because it uses an interdisciplinary approach which does not fall into the artificial created disciplinary categories (Rabaka 2016). Of course, the phenomenological experience of being inside and seeing the reality through the window is not necessarily the full reality (Zizek, Living in the End Times 2011). Nonetheless, I consider it important for the field of IIL and for the ongoing academic discussions in the critical theory of International Law to pursue this work. In this sense, I challenge the reader to have an epistemic openness and not to reject this work *a priori* without reading the whole book.

The intervention made by this book aims at contributing towards the advancement of knowledge in the study of International Investment Law (IIL). In doing so, the novelty of this book relies on four important aspects:

- In using altogether, the vectors of coloniality, development, capitalism, neoliberalism and power to problematise the IIL system showing how it operates as an instrument that facilitates situations of systemic violence.
- In using post-war critical thought, especially southern perspectives chiefly outlined by Fanon, Lewis Gordon, Oscar Guardiola-Rivera, Ha-Joon Chang and Enrique Dussel among others to analyse and problematise the IIL system.
- In the methodology proposed for the problematisation of the pursuance of the inwardly critical inquiry, which is a cross-road between genealogy, historical materialism and a historical, political, economic and legal analysis, which can also be used inwardly enquires not only for the IIL system but also for other branches of International Economic Law. It is historical materialism in the sense put forward by Walter Benjamin in his take on the historiographical method inspired by the likes of Aby Warburg and also in the historiographical approaches of Jane Ana and Lewis R. Gordon, that resists the classical historical approach, flagging up past events of danger (Benjamin 2007, 255–256) (Gordon and Gordon, A Companion to African-American Studies 2006) (Becker 2013). It is a political-economic analysis with a jurisprudential account of international law, in the sense used by Sundhya Pahuja in her doctoral thesis, showing the `postcolonial', economic and `political' qualities of the IIL system (Pahuja, Decolonising International Law: Development, Economic Growth And The Politics Of Universality 2008).

The reader must bear in mind that, this work neither intends to offer a blue print in the form of answers and clear solutions to the problems identified, nor to picture IIL as something evil. Rather this work intends to focus on the incompleteness of this institutional system and to intensify the reader's awareness as to the dangers surrounding the IIL system leaving the reader with questions and highlighting the fact that the IIL system requires serious attention to its current functioning, as its practices facilitate systemic violence.[8] In this form, this work hopes to encourage further research on the past and present of IIL and the form of how it works and relates with countries and individuals.

It is also important to highlight that although this work contains references to past events, they are presented in the context of historical events that are in constant change affecting our present (Koopman 2013). This approach differs from a mere historical approach that is an outward study, only linking patterns of change in the interactions of individuals (Appadurai, Modernity at Large: Cultural Dimensions of Globalisation 1996). It is also important to highlight the fact that this book does not hide the role that developing countries have played in the consolidation of the IIL system and the fact that, for instance, there are south to south IIA. Nonetheless and as previously mentioned and as is explained in the following chapters, the impact of the IIL system and IIA is different in developed countries than to developing countries for economic and budgetary reasons.

It is important to highlight the fact that this work finds itself closer to critical approaches presented by academics such as Kate Miles (Miles, The Origins of International Investment Law: Empire, Environment and the Safeguard of Capital 2013), Amanda Perry-Kessaris (Perry-Kessaris 2008), David Schneiderman (Schneiderman, Resisting Economic Globalisation: Critical Theory and International Investment Law 2013), M. Sornarajah (M. Sornarajah, The International Law on Foreign Investment 2010), Celine Tan (Faundez and Tan 2010), Andrew Lang (Lang 2011), Nicolas Perrone (Perrone 2016) or Rene Urueña who also pursue interdisciplinary research on the IIL system (Urueña 2012). In this sense, this work highlights the need to take an interdisciplinary approach to problematise the IIL system. The interdisciplinary approach taken in this project has allowed me to pursue a deeper and a broader analysis of the system, problematising it and questioning its history, functioning, institutions and effects by removing its veil of objective, neutral, apolitical and beneficial effects for Third-World host countries.

The methodology used in this research moves away from positivistic, more traditional and non-problematic methodologies that seek scientific

---

[8] Michel Foucault in an interview clarified that negative and dangerous are not the same. See Michel Foucault, 'On the Genealogy of Ethics: An Overview of Work in Progress', in Paul Rabinow (ed), *The Foucault Reader* (Pantheon Books 1984), 343.

objectivity. In doing so, I show my discontent with the traditional approach that 'requires the reduction of the individual scholar and student so that she is subordinated to a collective technical endeavour' and which is '"anchored" by concrete accumulations of data', and the market nihilism and requirements (J. A. Gordon 2006, 280).

The use of this alternative methodology is not an evasion from traditional research methodology, but instead is the result of growing awareness concerning the limitations of traditional methodologies for the pursuance of this project. Arguably, this trans-disciplinary methodology could also be used in the theorisation and problematisation of other bodies of International Economic Law.

It is important to highlight at this point the fact that although this work uses a North-South framework, nowadays, there are North-to-North and South-to-South treaties for the protection and promotion of foreign investments such as the Comprehensive Economic and Trade Agreement (CETA) between Canada and the European Union or the Bilateral Investment Treaty (BIT) between Colombia and Peru. However, this current reality cannot hide the past of the IIL system as an instrument in the context of North–South relationships. The global socio-economic situation, whereby existing differences between developed and developing countries, the societies most affected by the limitations imposed by the IIL system are the peripheral countries must also be considered.

It is also important to clarify at this point the use of the term 'Third World' in this book, which was originally coined by the anti-colonial scholar Alfred Savuy (Pahuja, Decolonising International Law: Development, Economic Growth and the Politics of Universality 2011), refers to the group of countries that were former colonies and which share socio-economic problems in terms of infrastructure, industrialisation, poverty, living standards, among others. The term 'Third World' is also used in this work in a symbolic way in order to represent a political project of resistance and struggle pursued by the peoples of Africa, Asia and Latin America, all seeking for a better present and a brighter future, reformulating the current socio-economic structures that are the result of the colonial past (Sauvy 1952).

Moreover, the use of the term 'Third World' is not constant and other terms such as peripheral, poor, developing, non-industrialised and capital importer are also used. All the mentioned terms are interchangeable, placed throughout this project as a substitute of the term 'Third World'. The interchangeable use of terms is not simply a mistake. Rather, it has been done intentionally so as to capture the fact that a socio-economic division that came out of the colonial system, and which has been transformed over time using different labels, has continued throughout the time. The point of such language usage is to insist on the constitutive and contemporary character of such divisions throughout modernity/coloniality.

Along this same line, it is important to clarify that throughout this book, the reader will find the use of the term 'West'. In the context of this book, the term 'West' is used to refer to a fictional label that represents the bloc of Western European countries, Canada and the USA. The term 'West' sometimes is also interchanged in the text for terms such as rich, developed, industrialised, or capital exporting countries (Piketty 2014).

Accordingly, this book is divided into six (6) chapters that problematise the production of 'truths' surrounding the IIL system. Chapter 1 claims that the IIL system as an instrument that operates within the capitalist system, with an encrypted discourse, influenced by a neoliberal ideology and rooted to the colonial past, configures itself as an instrument that facilitates situations of international systemic violence. The analysis is pursued from the perspective of global inequalities and the negative consequences for local communities caused by the IIL system.

Chapter 2 offers an analysis from a political-economy perspective on the whereabouts of Foreign Direct Investment (FDI). In doing so, the chapter approaches the relationship between investors and states within a framework of global capitalist market discussing the reasons for a capitalist to invest abroad as part of the capitalist logic of accumulating more. This chapter lays the groundwork by providing necessary context to the non-specialised as well as the specialised reader so as to enjoy the book.

Chapter 3 analyses the main clauses common to BITs (or investor's chapters within FTAs) – as well as to Investor State Dispute Settlement (ISDS) that are the essential elements to understanding the impact of IIL system. Chapter 4 explores the tensions that exist between the encryption of the IIL discourse, the host state, the home state and foreign investors. Accordingly, this chapter argues that the encryption of the IIL discourse contributes to maintaining patterns of epistemic superiority and power that began in colonial times and which continues to happen in the present day.

Chapter 5 analyses neoliberalism from the stand point of an ideological project that affects the intellectual subconscious of individuals that give shape and form to the IIL system. Finally, chapter 6 argues that some important changes within the IIL, which have been regarded as positive, are nothing more than actions adopted by the system itself to continue its existence and as such perpetuating itself. In order to develop the presented argument, this chapter uses the analytical tool of autopoiesis (following Niklas Luhman) to analyse the operation of the IIL as a self-contained system that re-enacts and perpetuates itself. A system is autopoietic when it 'reproduces its own elements through their interaction' (Rottleuthner 1988, 114).

Finally, I would like to thank Lewis R. Gordon, Oscar Guardiola-Rivera and all the Birkbeck community for the supportive and vibrant environment they provided that allowed me to conclude this book.

Chapter 1

Systemic Violence and International Investment Law

'The basic confrontation which seemed to be colonialism versus anti-colonialism, indeed capitalism versus socialism, is already losing importance. What matters today, the issue which blocks the horizon, is the need for a redistribution of wealth. Humanity will have to address this question, no matter how devastating the consequences may be.' (F. Fanon 2004, 55)

INTRODUCTION

This first chapter of this book seeks to take the reader along on a journey of questioning the International Investment Law system (IIL) from the perspective of systemic violence. Therefore, the main argument presented in this chapter is that the IIL system is an international legal structure that facilitates situations of international systemic violence. Of course, I am aware that linking IIL with violence may generate discomfort among readers, especially for those close to the system. However, I shall clarify this controversial argument in the paragraphs which follow.

It is nevertheless important to draw attention to the fact that the arguments presented in this chapter must be read closely with the rest of the book. The reader must be aware that what makes the IIL an instrument that facilitates systemic violence is that the system is encrypted and autopoietic. Furthermore, it is framed by a neoliberal ideology and the developmentalism discourse that serves to legitimise it, hiding its colonial roots and its negative effects upon communities in general.

It is also important to bear in mind that the argument presented in this chapter does not hide the reality that physical violence still occurs within the context of controlling natural resources and that this could involve domestic and foreign interests. For instance, the conflict that has engulfed Congo for years has been 'mainly about access to, control of and trade in five key mineral resources: coltan, diamonds, copper, cobalt and gold'. The situation in Congo has benefited warlords as well as foreign companies (Zizek, Living In The End Times 2011, 163). However, this chapter focuses on the role of IIL system as instrument that facilitates systemic violence.

Hannah Arendt points out that violence and its problems are issues that tend to remain obscure because people are usually reluctant to approach them (Arendt 1970). One of the main challenges regarding the study and analysis of violence is that the concept is usually limited to physical violence in which there is a clear perpetrator and a victim (Zizek, Violence 2009). However, to shed light on the topic of violence within the dynamics of the twentieth and twenty-first centuries, it is necessary to analyse violence beyond the common approach. Accordingly, I will analyse IIL as an instrument that facilitates systemic violence by taking that broader approach.

Above all, it is important to not forget that colonialism was primarily a form of economic domination and exploitation of "the other" using political and legal instruments (Cabral 2016, 91). In the post-colonial scenario of the second half of the twentieth century, different 'tactics', visible and less visible, have been used by former colonial powers to overcome the challenges of the new political reality whereby former colonial countries became independent countries.

Those tactics aimed at maintaining long-lasting conditions of alienation, subordination and control over former colonies by retaining a certain degree of control and directly interfering with the autonomous domestic decision-making processes of Third World countries (Angie 2007, 105) (Nkrumah 1965, 243). It is important to remember that, from the second half of the twentieth century onwards, developing countries have been subjects of an ambiguous agenda to incorporate them to the global economy (Faundez and Tan 2010).

Examples of visible tactics have included the establishment of military bases in the new-born states, deployment in the field of technocrat advisers or the support of internal groups (legal or illegal) for regime change as in the case of Chile or Nicaragua, among others (Nkrumah 1965) (Guardiola-Rivera, 2013). Examples of less-visible tactics have included forms of developmental aid (either coming from a country or from a multilateral international financial institution), high interest loans or the persuading of Third World countries to enter international treaties designed within a framework of North-South relationships as is the case of International Investment Agreements (IIA) (Nkrumah 1965) (Guardiola-Rivera, 2010).

Within this context, the IIL system has become an instrument for the exercise of legal, political and economic influence world-wide but having special effects upon Third World countries. The developmentalism discourse combined with a neoliberal ideology has created a framework for the legitimisation and promotion of the IIL system as an essential element by which periphery countries may reach the 'promised land' of development. Moreover, the disparity that continues to exist between North and South brings up ongoing questions as to the effectiveness of the IIL system in promoting economic growth and conveying countries to that promised land of development, and hence, reducing global disparity.

The domination of the IIL system is based on the ability today of Western powers to write the world's history whilst suppressing colonial histories. The discourse of peace and depoliticisation that backs the IIL system conceals situations of systemic violence created by the system. Furthermore, western powers continue to have an interest in maintaining their domestic markets which are based upon limitless consumption. This requires supply of the surplus from the periphery, but at the same time, it affects the environment and the lives of thousands of humans (Wood 2016).

In the development of the argument I use relevant theorists who have approached the issue of violence from different perspectives such as Frantz Fanon, Hussein Abdilahi Bulhan, Slavoj Zizek, Paul Farmer and Johan Galtung. Their broader approach to violence facilitates an understanding of how the IIL system facilitates situations of international systemic violence which have a direct impact on the social, psychological and physical integrity of citizens of non-industrialised countries. This impact includes restraining, among other things, opportunities for social improvement, economic growth and protection of the environment and culture. It is important not to lose sight that economic domination, promotion of unequal trade, plunder of resources, cultural, political and economic intervention in peripheral societies pursued by capital exporter countries and MNCs, among others, are also situations that amount to violence (Bulhan 1985, 380).

FROM PLUNDER TO THE IIL SYSTEM?

Plunder was one of the central organising activities during the colonial period. Plunder was also a right derived not only from the Western might but also from the "civilisation" that the West brought to the uncivilised "other" that inhabited colonial territories (Mattei and Nader 2008). Plundering was performed through force and physical violence and was used to maintain the limitless extraction of resources in the periphery that were shipped directly to colonial centres thus, sustaining the economy of the metropolis.[1] In this regard, Laura Nader and Ugo Mattei note the following:

> Plunder has always been one of the most important ways of primitive accumulation of capital, an accumulation which, after the Middle Ages, made possible a new historical stage in the world economic evolution. (Mattei and Nader 2008, 107)

The interest of appropriation of natural resources by the West, linked to colonial and imperial practices, continued after the end of the Second World War. Although former colonies became politically and legally independent countries, they continued being *de facto* dependent. This dependence is presented under the umbrella of a free global market exchange instead of in the form of direct servitude (Zizek, Living In The End Times 2011, 290). Furthermore, the existing inequalities that transcended the colonial period forced Third World countries to allow the extraction and plunder of their natural resources so as to later purchase manufactured products at twice the price of those raw materials.

Principle four (4) of the Atlantic Charter, signed by British Prime Minister Winston Churchill and U.S. President Franklin D. Roosevelt, expresses the interests of these Western countries in having access to the raw materials that were required for an economic prosperity:

> They will endeavor with due respect for their existing obligations, to further enjoyment by all States, great or small, victor or vanquished, of access, on equal terms, to the trade and to the raw materials of the world which are needed for their economic prosperity. (Churchill & Roosevelt, 1941)

The extraction of raw materials has historically benefited Western Economies and not so clearly peripheral countries (Nkrumah 1965, 84). Raw materials are essential to the production of manufactured goods, and thus become an essential element for the functioning of the consumption-based Western economy. Regarding this aspect, Keith Aoki states the following:

> The pattern is becoming depressingly familiar: resources flow out of the Southern regions and are transformed by Northern entrepreneurial authors and inventors into intellectual properties, which in many cases are priced so high that the people from whom such knowledge originated cannot afford to license them. (Keith Aoki 1998, 26–27)

---

[1] Dichotomy coined by CEPAL in the construction of the theory of dependency.

The continuity of this economic relationship of extracting raw materials in the periphery to be later transformed in the West has contributed to maintaining the gaps and inequalities that began during the colonial period. Countries producing manufactured goods, for which the returns are higher, play better in the global market compared to others that export raw materials required for the production of the manufactured goods but which have a lower return.

Foreign investment has been deemed to be essential to a country's economic development. As such, the best option for an underdeveloped country to become 'developed', would be to attract as much foreign investment as possible. However, as discussed in the following chapters, the economic benefits for the host country are not clear. What is clear is that foreign investments allow the transfer of surplus and profit at a world-wide level (Dussel 2014, 60). It is also clear that, Foreign Direct Investment (FDI), as one type of foreign investment, impacts the relations between different actors, sellers, employers, employees, consumers, producers, among others, at world-wide level (Perry-Kessaris 2008).

Linking FDI with development has allowed the legitimisation of practices of plunder that started under colonial structures and which have continued following the 'independence' or 'decolonisation' processes (Subhashini 2002). Development has also naturalised the importance of non-resistance, based upon the consensus (and the opinion) of the importance of taking all the necessary steps to reach the 'promised land of development'.

Additionally, linking FDI and development, kicked off a race to the bottom among Third World countries to gain the most foreign investment, adopting measures that facilitated even more intensively the extraction of resources and the activity of MNCs. Neoliberal reforms that began in the 1990s created a more favourable and friendlier environment for FDI in Third World countries, especially in extractive industries (Hinojosa and Bebbington 2010, 222). It is important to highlight the fact that most of the FDI in Third World countries assumes the form of resource seeking investment. Thus, the IIL system operates as a mechanism that facilitates the appropriation of natural resources, whilst failing to tackle the inequality that exists between industrialised and non-industrialised countries (Pahuja 2011, 138).

Both factors, the competition among Third World countries plus the hegemonisation of neoliberal ideology played out favourably for the consolidation of the IIL system as a necessary and important world-wide law system. The increased number of IIA that include Free Trade Agreements (FTA) with investment provisions and Bilateral Investment Treaties (BITs) (389 and 2895, respectively, as of 2020) (UN Conference on Trade and Development, 2020, p. 106) and the consolidation of institutions such as the International Center for Settlement of Investment Disputes (ICSID) and the International Chamber of Commerce (ICC) as Investor-State Dispute Settlement (ISDS) forums for the resolution of conflicts via arbitration between host states and foreign investors are manifestations of such consolidation.

FTA and BITs have permeated world trade relations offering enhanced protection for the activities of foreign investors in host countries, even over local interests. This network of international treaties limits the ability of host countries, especially peripheral countries, to regulate aspects of common interest such as environment, socio-economic needs or human rights. In addition, the public finances of Third World countries can suffer important knocks because of the elevated costs associated with investment arbitral procedures.

Limiting the ability of host states to regulate translates into contributing to the continuity and legalisation of the plunder of local resources, a process that originated in colonial times, which occurs without consideration of the public interest, human rights or environmental protection. And all this is endured regardless of the fact that the hoped for trickle-down of the economic benefits into the economy at large has yet to be proved.

The econo centric discourse surrounding the IIL system presents IIA and arbitral tribunals as instruments that facilitate transactions and the functioning of the market, but it hides its violent effects (Perry-Kessaris 2008). Whilst IIL imposes limitations upon host countries, however, it offers foreign investors extra legal protection at many different levels. Foreign investors are protected not only by domestic regulation but also by all the IIA network. Foreign investors can also count on the protection of international agencies such as the Multilateral Investment Guarantee Agency (MIGA) or the U.S. Overseas Private Investment Corporation (Perry-Kessaris 2008). Additionally, and as presented in greater detail in the following chapters, the IIL system lacks accountability, not only due to its encryption but also due to the fact that awards can be kept secret by the request of the parties.

IIL is applauded for protecting foreign investor's interests and business activities whilst challenging the sovereign power of states. It is also applauded as it serves to attract foreign investors to countries having the expectation this investment will contribute over the long haul to attain the goal of development. However, and as already noted, the economic benefits to host countries are not clear since the legal and economic needs of foreign investor are granted priority over community rights, human rights, environmental rights (Perry-Kessaris 2008).

FDI AND INVESTMENTS AWARDS: SOME DATA

In 2019, Global foreign direct investment (FDI) totalled US$1.54 trillion (United Nations Conference on Trade and Development 2020). The top twenty FDI home economies for 2019 were the following:

Japan	United Kingdom
United States	Italy
Netherlands	Spain
China	Sweden
Germany	Russian Federation
Canada	Belgium
Hong Kong, China	Ireland
France	Denmark
Republic of Korea	United Arab Emirates
Singapore	Brazil

The above data confirms that developed economies continue to dominate the FDI market. This trend has been no different in comparison with the years 2015 (United Conference on Trade and Development 2016); 2010 (United Conference on Trade and Development 2011); 2005 (United Nations Conference on Trade and Development 2006); or 2000 (United Conference on Trade and Development 2001).

It is also important to highlight that in terms of Gross Domestic Product (GDP), the United States, China, Japan, Germany, India, the United Kingdom, France, Italy, Brazil, Canada, Russia, South Korea, Spain, Australia, Mexico, Indonesia, Netherlands, Saudi Arabia, Turkey and Switzerland are the twenty largest economies in the world (The World Bank 2019), (Silver 2020).[2] Out of these twenty countries, the top ten countries account for 66 per cent of the economy of the world. It is important to highlight that this list of countries has not changed greatly since the 1980s (Silver 2020).

UNCTAD's data shows that in terms of investment awards, from 1987 to 31 December 2019, there have been 1,023 known treaty-based ISDS cases (United Nations Conference on Trade and Development 2020).[3] Out of the 1,023 cases, 246 have been decided in favour of the state, 198 in favour of the investor, 139 settled cases, 77 discontinued cases and 14 cases in which liability was

---

[2] U.S. Nominal GDP: $21.44 trillion – U.S. GDP (PPP): $21.44 trillion; China Nominal GDP: $14.14 trillion – China GDP (PPP): $27.31 trillion; (Japan Nominal GDP: $5.15 trillion – Japan GDP (PPP): $5.75 trillion); Germany Nominal GDP: $3.86 trillion – Germany GDP (PPP): $4.44 trillion); India Nominal GDP: $2.94 trillion-India GDP (PPP): $10.51 trillion; U.K. Nominal GDP: $2.83 trillion – U.K. GDP (PPP): $3.04 trillion; France Nominal GDP: $2.71 trillion – France GDP (PPP): $2.96 trillion; Italy Nominal GDP: $1.99 trillion – Italy GDP (PPP): $2.40 trillion; Brazil Nominal GDP: $1.85 trillion – Brazil GDP (PPP): $3.37 trillion; Canada Nominal GDP: $1.73 trillion – Canada GDP (PPP): $1.84 trillion; Russia Nominal GDP: $1.64 trillion – Russia GDP (PPP): $4.21 trillion; South Korea Nominal GDP: $1.63 trillion – South Korea GDP (PPP): $2.14 trillion; Spain Nominal GDP: $1.4 trillion – Spain GDP (PPP): $1.86 trillion; Australia Nominal GDP: $1.38 trillion – Australia GDP (PPP): $1.32 trillion; Mexico Nominal GDP: $1.22 trillion – Mexico GDP (PPP): $2.57 trillion; Indonesia Nominal GDP: $1.11 trillion – Indonesia GDP (PPP): $3.50 trillion; Netherlands Nominal GDP: $902.36 billion – Netherlands GDP (PPP): $969.23 billion; Saudi Arabia Nominal GDP: $779.29 billion – Saudi Arabia GDP (PPP): $1.86 trillion; Turkey Nominal GDP: $743.71 billion – Turkey GDP (PPP): $2.29 trillion; Switzerland Nominal GDP: $715.36 billion – Switzerland GDP (PPP): $548.48 billion.

[3] Pending 343, concluded 674, unknown 6.

found but no damages awarded (UN Conference on Trade and Development 2020). Adding cases ruled in favour of the investor and settled cases (the settlement means that the state reaches an agreement that settles the investor's claims), the total number of cases that has evidently favoured the investor's interests are 337. From the 1,023 known treaty-based ISDS cases, 550 have been cases against developing countries, including LDCs (53.7 per cent), out of which 119 have been ruled in favour of the states (21.6 per cent) and only 295 cases have been against developed countries, out of which 90 were resolved in favoured of the host state (30.5 per cent) (United Nations Conference on Trade and Development 2020).

In a previous study carried out by Susan Franck in which she analysed 102 public awards up to 1 June 2006, she found that most investment claims were brought by companies from developed states. Her conclusions were as follows:

> Investors making claims predominantly hailed from developed states. The United States had the largest number of investors making such claims, but countries such as Italy, Canada, Spain, France, the Netherlands and the United Kingdom also had large numbers of investors. Out of a total of 107 investors, ninety-five (88.9%) investors were from OECD countries. Coding investors' country of origin by the World Bank's country classification system, 27 yielded similar results. Nearly 90% of claims were brought from investors in 'high income' countries. Interestingly, there were no investors from 'low income' countries as defined by the World Bank or from LDCs as defined by the United Nations. (Franck 2007–2008).

In the same study, Franck found that most cases (45 per cent) were against upper middle-income countries (according to the World Bank classification). This type of country included Argentina, Bulgaria, Chile, Kazakhstan, Latvia, Malaysia, Mexico, Poland, Romania, Russia, Slovakia, Turkey and Venezuela (Franck 2007–2008). Another important number of claims were against 'lower middle income' countries (28 per cent). In this band were countries such as Albania, Bolivia, Ecuador, Egypt, Jordan, Moldova, Morocco, Paraguay, Peru, the Philippines, Sri Lanka and Ukraine 8.5 per cent of the claims were against 'low income' countries including Burundi and Kyrgyzstan (Franck 2007–2008).

IIL AS INSTRUMENT OF SYSTEMIC VIOLENCE

IIL is an asymmetric system that puts into question whether the expected unqualified benefits to developing countries in fact occur. It also creates ambiguity in the sense that although the text of the treaty reflects equality as between the parties the reality differs (Faundez and Tan 2010). The data presented demonstrates that developing countries do not invest at the same level as developed countries. It also obscures the fact that the legal costs inherent to the system may deter foreign investors from developing countries from bringing a legal claim against a developed host state.

IIA are the result of economic, political and diplomatic negotiations in which the strongest states (capital exporting states) secure the best terms in investment treaties for the protection of their industries (Wong 2009). In doing so, these treaties judicialise international economic relations by imposing a form of global governance standardising the way in which foreign investors should be treated, and which no not necessarily reflect the normative and political needs of developing countries. In this regard, Kate Miles says:

> [H]istorical alignment of state interests with those of foreign investors, and in particular with those of the trading companies, together with their influence over the development of international property rules, meant that those laws represented the interests of capital-exporting states and their nationals. (Miles 2010)

Under this logic, it is possible to affirm that the protection offered to private individuals and companies by the IIL system, resembles the dynamics of colonial times. These dynamics are characterised by a close relationship between the economic interests of colonial centres and private entrepreneurs such as the East Indian Company (HEIC) or the Dutch East Indian Company (VOC).

It is important to reflect on the fact that developing countries were incorporated as dependent subjects into an international legal system over whose design they had limited influence (F. Fanon 2004). In addition, it is important to reflect on the fact that, as result of the global market dynamics, developing countries continue to be marginalised from decision-making places within the IIL system, this rendering it difficult for them to redress the asymmetry. In other words, developing countries transform themselves into rule takers rather than agents of important change of the IIL system.

Furthermore, and as will be explained in more detail in the following chapters, the structure of the IIL system grants to investment arbitrators the power and the strength to persuade and coerce host states and their civil servants to act or not to act. This power is derived from the authority granted by the IIA that invests them with the capacity to legally assess acts *jure imperii* and to decrypt the encrypted system. The authority and the legitimacy of the arbitrators to decrypt the system are almost unchallengeable and unquestioned and requires obedience from the other players. Of course, this obedience is accepted by states when ratifying IIA. As stated by Zizek:

> Authority thus does not stem merely from the attributes of individuals. Its exercise depends on a willingness on *the part of others* to grant respect and legitimacy, rather than one´s personal ability to persuade or coerce. (Zizek, Living In The End Times 2011, 388)

Any form of criticism is presented as resistance to progress and, as such, amounts to resistance to development becoming a serious threat to the economic stability of the state. Under such circumstances, understanding IIL and its effects requires to go beyond the orthodox approach to violence which we associate with forms of physical force by one individual against other. Slavoj Zizek observes that the word violence usually brings to the mind common signs of visible and physical violence such as crime, civil unrest, armed conflict, among other things, in which not only the action but also the victim and the perpetrator are identifiable (Zizek 2009). This conceptualisation of violence associated with physical violence is the most common approach and is present in the works of different scholars and institutions that deal with the issue of violence.

For instance, Graeme Newman and Marvin E. Wolfgang are among behaviour scientists that reinforce a conceptualisation of violence restricted to harmful physical force by one person against another. Graeme Newman defines 'violence' in the following way: 'that which leads to physical injury or damage, since historically it is the only aspect of violence that we are able to observe or record' (Newman 1971, 2).

Wolfgang in the same way conceptualises violence as follows:

> I shall use the term 'violence' to refer to the intentional use of physical force on another person or noxious physical stimuli invoked by one person on another. The physical force may be viewed as assaultive, designed to cause pain or injury as an end in itself. (Wolfgang 1976)

The Violence Prevention Alliance (VPA), which is a network of the World Health Organisation (WHO), also approaches violence from the point of view of physical force. It defines violence in the following way:

> [T]he intentional use of physical force or power, threatened or actual, against oneself, another person, or against a group or community, that either results in or has a high likelihood of resulting in injury, death, psychological harm, underdevelopment, or deprivation. (Violence Prevention Alliance n.d.)

Beyond a limited approach to violence, limiting it to physical force, Frantz Fanon, Bulhan, Galtung, Paul Framer and Zizek, are among other scholars who have worked on theories of forms of non-physical violence linked to the configuration of the capitalist economic system and its colonial and imperial past. In the following section I will briefly analyse their approaches as a foreword to the discussion of systemic violence within the context of IIL.

Frantz Fanon, identified the existence of a form of structural violence, that is characterised by promising rights, progress, equality and stability but falls short in fulfilling those promises to the 'other' (Gordon 2017, 50–51). This form of violence, as presented in his celebrated book "The Wretched of the Earth", is the result of the capitalist economic structure shaped by the colonial past. Fanon was aware that in the post-colonial context the effects of colonisation would still have their effects upon the newly independent nations. This meant that the economic disparity shaped by the colonial and imperial past, would be difficult to overcome through the decolonisation of the Third World if radical structural changes were not made (F. Fanon 2004).

Fanon shows the reader that the conditions created by the colonial and imperial past create an economic situation whereby Third World countries, surrendered to the developmentalism discourse, sought to attain a development level similar to that reached by former colonial centres (F. Fanon 2004, 55). The former colonial centres, took advantage of their power advantage might, which was itself a result of their colonial and imperial past. Fanon also warned about how the dynamics of capitalism (as well as socialism) were becoming obstacles for Third World countries:

> The basic issue with which we are faced is not the unequivocal choice between socialism and capitalism such as they have been defined by men from different continents and different periods of time. We know, of course, that the capitalist way of life is incapable of allowing us to achieve our national and universal project. Capitalist exploitation, the cartels and monopolies, are the enemies of underdeveloped countries. (F. Fanon 2004, 55–56)

In this context, Fanon can be read as making the reader aware that the economic situation experienced on a daily basis by Third World countries is necessarily linked to its colonial past. This situation has left governments, in a globalised market, with fewer economic choices which then translates into a continuity of international economic policies of subordination including the acceptance of unbalanced economic treaties.

Building upon Frantz Fanon's understanding of violence at the international level, which most of his critics and many of his sympathetic readers have hitherto ignored, violence includes the existence of a system of norms through which something wrong or undeserved and unjust, happens. This distinguishes it from mere force or the exercise of military and physical force (Gordon 2017, 51). It also signifies, that a dishonouring of legitimate expectations raised by the existence of a system of rules and norms, such as the post-war and allegedly post-colonial context being based on equality and self-determination of countries, also creates a scenario of violence (Gordon 2017, 51) (Hathaway and Shapiro 2017).

Hussein Abdilahi Bulhan in his analysis of Fanon also highlights that violence and peace are not only about armaments but also about matters of economics and of the psychological effects of confrontation, relations of recognition and non-relations, as well as of domination and influence (Bulhan 1985). Specifically, Bulhan is critical about the interdependence of countries in terms of economic and politics and the psyches:

> This interdependence in economics and politics also entails an interdependence of psyches. Thus the global problem of war and peace is not merely a question of armaments or economics, but also a problem of psyches confronting, dominating and influencing each other. More significantly, this global interdependence is based neither on reciprocity nor on equality. It so happens that the wealth of a given set of countries depends on the impoverishment of others... This nonreciprocal, imposed interdependence in which some gain and others lose, some thrive and others suffer is not an inevitable, natural order. (Bulhan 1985, 38)

The restricted approach to the concept of violence (limited to the use of physical force), leaves on the outside acts such as the plunder of land and resources, the impoverishment of society and social oppression created by international market forces, and the worsening of the environment and the health of populations. For Bulhan, violence occurs when conditions inhibit human potential:

> Violence is any relation, process or condition by which an individual or a group violates the physical, social and/or psychological integrity of another person or group. From this perspective, violence inhibits human growth, negates inherent potential, limits productive living and causes death. (Bulhan 1985, 135)

Bulhan continues, affirming that violence within the system allows unequal distribution among members of society becomes the most lethal form of violence, endorsed by authorities and which presents itself as the natural order. In this regard, Bulhan mentions the following: 'A situation of oppression rests primarily on structural violence which in turn fosters institutional, interpersonal, and intrapersonal violence' (Bulhan 1985, 135).

Paul Farmer identifies how history and economic structures work as elements that constrain the agency of individuals by generating situations of personal suffering among those so constrained thus, generating a structural violence (Farmer 1996). In his work, Farmer identifies how those most affected by structural violence are the world's poorest who are also the most likely not to have a voice or choice; rather they follow the faith imposed by the structure, led by few and their interests (Farmer 1996).

Johan Galtung, points out that in order to take action to address the variety of problems affecting society it is necessary to think of the concept of violence in different dimensions. Galtung talks about a broader approach towards violence, observing that

> highly unacceptable social orders would still be compatible with peace. Hence, an extended concept of violence is indispensable but that concept should be a logical extension, not merely a list of undesirables. (Galtung 1969)

For Galtung, violence occurs when an avoidable act has the ability to reduce the potential somatic and mental realisations of a human or group of human beings. In this regard, Gaultung states the following:

> Violence is present when human beings are being influenced so that their actual somatic and mental realizations are below their potential realizations…In other words, when the potential is higher, then the actual is by definition avoidable, and when it is avoidable, then violence is present. (Galtung 1969, 167, 169)

According to Zizek subjective violence consists of the type of violence in which one subject uses physical force against another (Zizek 2009). Zizek states that subjective violence is only one form of violence among a variety of forms of violence that includes verbal violence, symbolic violence or systemic violence in which physical force does not play an important role but still also affects millions of people. In this regard Zizek states the following:

> [V]iolence is not a direct property of some acts but is distributed between acts and their contexts; sometimes a polite smile can be more violent than a brutal outburst. (Zizek 2009, 180)

Zizek continues, arguing that besides subjective violence, there is also an objective violence which is a form of violence created by the capitalist economic system and is characterised as no longer being attributable to a specific individual but which is systemic, objective and anonymous (Zizek 2009). Systemic violence appears as one form of objective violence and is the direct consequence of the political and economic system (Zizek 2009).

For Zizek, systemic violence (as a form of objective violence) is assumed by individuals as a normal condition, becoming invisible to the eyes of the society. The invisibility of violence to the eyes of the population is described by Zizek as follows:

> Systemic Violence is thus something like the notorious 'dark matter' of physics, the counterpart to an all-too-visible subjective violence. (Zizek 2009)

Harry Van Der Linden comments on Zizek's aproach to systemic violence as follows:

> The agents of systemic violence, to the contrary, do not generate or use 'force', but rather create or maintain institutional rules that unjustly restrict the opportunities of their victims. (Linden 2012)

In this context, systemic violence is characterised by the limited or unnecesary use of force. Rather, the main element is the imposition or maintenance of unfair social conditions for individuals within a society.

Non-physical forms of violence, require normative systems to justify wrongdoings that cause degradation to human beings (Linden 2012). The fact that other forms of violence can be less evident, whereby the victim and the perpetrator are not easily identifiable, can lead those forms of violence to create more negative effects than the subjective form of violence (Zizek 2009). Normalisation deters any possibility of overcoming a form of violence which could affect millions of individuals around the world.

Considering the foregoing works, my understanding of systemic violence is the creation and maintenance of unbalanced legal, economic and political conditions, that have a direct impact on the social, psychological and phsycial integrity of citizens of non-industrialised countries, restraining, among other things, opportunities for social improvement, economic growth and protection of enviroment and culture. Systemic violence relies upon international structures that count on their own networks, ideologies and institutions. International systemic violence is embodied and promoted by the system, making it invisible to those affected by it; on the contrary, it is seen as the *status quo*.

In the specific case of the IIL, this system serves as an instrument that facilitates systemic violence as it limits the ability of host peripheral countries to regulate matters of public interest whenever they affect the economic interests of foreign investors. IIL gives priority to the economic interests of private parties over the interests of the community in general at an exaggerated level. The system helps to naturalise exploitation, domination and violence via the ideas of equality of states and investment as a path to development. Foreign investors, protected by IIA, travel the world finding cheaper labour, more flexible norms and lower taxes, among other things.

It is also to highlight the fact that the IIL system exploits catastrophes and difficult situations in all countries but especially in developing countries. For instance, the case of Argentina in which the government response to the crisis was the trigger for multiple legal claims filed by foreign investors against the host state. There was also the case of Uruguay responding to the increase of smokers in the country. In this case, the order to use blank packaging for all the cigarette trademarks, as a measure to reduce cigarette consumption was also the trigger for a foreign investor claim against the country.

It is also important to mention that in the current situation of this pandemic caused by the Covid-19, academics and NGOs have called for a moratorium on IIA (Bacchus and Sachs 2020). However, such a call has been completely ignored by the system and the posible legal claims out of decisions adopted to protect the population will be challenged by foreign investors. We will have to wait the outcome of such claims including whether the Arbitral Investment Tribunals will accept arguments of necessity or *force majeure* as circumstances precluding the wrongfulness of the host state (International Law Commission 2001).

IIL, GLOBALCENTRISM AND SYSTEMIC VIOLENCE

In contrast to other branches of Public International Law (PIL), the novelty of the IIL system is that it positions states on a notionally equal footing with MNCs (and individuals), when acting as foreign investors, before offshore investment arbitral tribunals. This special situation allows foreign investors to use investment arbitration as a vehicle to persuade (or even coerce) host countries to behave or act economically, politically and legally in a way that is most convenient for their economic interests.

Although the links between governments and private interests continue to exist, the parallel equation according which the success of the private entrepreneur equals the success of the home country, is fading away. A variety of conditions in the global market have led corporations to abandon specific territorial spaces to create their own spaces and making the globe their jurisdiction. It is important not to forget that with the end of the 'American Century', multiple centres of global economic power have formed around the world (Zizek, Living in the End Times 2011).

It is in this context that MNCs used Western states to create and strengthen the legal web of international treaties in order to protect and secure their economic activity on a global scale. MNCs also use their lobbing and links (corporatocracy) in their home state to put pressure on other states to enter into international treaties that protect foreign investment (Pilkington 2016). On the other hand, MNCs put pressure on peripheral states to accept entry into IIA as well as in allowing MNCs, acting as foreign investors, to pursue their activities in the host country.

As can be seen in this new reality, MNCs use all their capabilities and power to create an international environment whereby they can invest worldwide safely and securely, whilst not depending on local courts and having the ability to challenge policies and regulatory powers of states (Salacuse and Sullivan 2009). Fernando Coronil suggests a move from Eurocentrism to Globalcentrism as a direct effect of the market that affects non-industrialised populations but also subordinated sectors within industrialised countries (Coronil 2000). In this new reality of a global market, all territories become subjects of interest to MCNs.

In this new framework, Western countries are also starting to experience the pressure and negative effects of the IIL system.[4] The IIL is also teaching lessons to Western countries about the functioning of the rule of the market on a global scale. Hence, a new form of Global Order is structured in which the real winners are the MNCs and the world's super rich. Whilst democracy is domestic, and we choose leaders to deal with domestic problems, the market, and investment moves on a global scale.

Considering the global socio-economic structure, any economic effect, especially those directly derived from IIL, can more greatly affect the weakest part of the population of the Global South (Baxi 2009). For developing countries, it is certainly difficult to fully comply with all the rules of International Economic Law especially as it restricts their ability to pursue policies suitable for their socio-economic needs (Faundez and Tan 2010). Furthermore, the economic impact of IIL on developing economies is higher than the impact in developed economies.

Fanon referring to the difference between proletariats in capitalist countries compared to the proletariat in a colonised country serves to emphasise on the different effects that an arbitral award could have on a developing country. In this respect Fanon stated the following:

> In the capitalist countries, the proletariat has nothing to lose and possibly everything to gain. In the colonized countries, the proletariat has everything to lose.
> (F. Fanon 2004, 64)

Fanon's approach in differentiating between the proletariat in the North and the South is useful to point out that despite the movements of global struggle,

---

[4] For instance, see the cases against Canada, Australia, or Germany, among others. Also see official reactions to the TTIP.

the global south will continue carrying a greater and heavier burden than those in the global north. The periphery has always been and will continue to be affected as result of the dynamics of the global capitalist markets through instruments such as the IIL system.

The whole IIL system creates the appropriate framework for instigating activities of plunder, coated with a sense of legality, putting aside the interests of entire populations and putting economic interests first. Paraphrasing Michael Foucault, market interests and its main players (foreign investors) have become one of the main reasons to confront governments and their laws (Foucault 2008, 247).

It is important to note at this point that the existing relationship in an arbitral tribunal between a foreign investor and a host state is asymmetrical as both parties are bound by different obligations. Whilst a country represents millions of people, the multinational company represents millions of dollars and the interests of shareholders. In this sense, what is happening is that MNCs making foreign investments can challenge any national or local law, administrative or judicial decision related to public welfare, human rights or economic regulation whenever it illegitimately affects the company's economic interests (Greider 2001). Of course, this scenario mirrors the colonial past in which the interests of privateers channelled through metropolis were prioritised over the rights of colonised communities. In this regard Kate Miles states the following:

> The impact of colonial 'otherness' can still be felt. These origins are responsible for the inherent investor bias of international investment law in the twentieth and twenty-first centuries. They find a modem manifestation in its excessive focus on investor rights, obsessive promotion of foreign investment to the exclusion of the interests of the host state and of other stakeholders, the manner in which it is used by foreign investors and their states to secure commercial interests, and the investor-state arbitral system of dispute resolution. (Miles 2010)

Even though the decisions reached by arbitration tribunals cannot overturn a national law, the awards cause an effect upon governments in the sense that it could be too expensive to adopt a policy or issue a norm if it affects the rights of investors; in other words, they can create a regulatory chill effect (Greider 2001). It is also important to mention that although the host state could obtain a favourable award, it does not mean that host governments are not affected by the trial itself. The investor's claims could have a significant importance not only on future decisions but also in host states, which will likely try to avoid future and expensive litigation (Bernasconi-Osterwalder and Weiss 2005; Miles, 2015).

For instance, the Indonesian government enacted regulations imposing obligations on mining companies to protect forests by forbidding open mining. In response to the new regulation, mining companies threatened the Indonesian government arguing that the regulations were in breach of BITs, forcing the Indonesian government to enact new legislation exempting mining companies previously holding such licences from the prohibition (Tienhaara 2006). Furthermore, entry into this type of treaty by peripheral countries can also lead to changes in internal legislation to comply with the requirements set out in these treaties. This process aims at the world-wide homogenisation of the rules for foreign investors, facilitating standardised global protection of their economic rights. An example of this situation is the 1999 amendment to the Colombian Constitution in order to comply with the requirements of the ILL system.

Before the amendment, Article 58 of the Colombian Constitution allowed expropriation without compensation, as an exceptional case, whenever the Colombian Congress deemed appropriate, and following parameters of public interest. As result of Article 58 different BITs signed by the Colombian government were affected. Thus, the government amended the 'problematic' article by drafting an article that always allowed payment of compensation upon expropriation without exception.

These simple examples show how the IIL system serves as an instrument to impose corporate interests and the will of a few upon the many. In the case of developing countries, the IIL system is based on an unbalanced legal, economic and political global structure. In addition, the IIL has a direct impact on the social, psychological and phsycial integrity of citizens of developing countries, restraining, among other things, opportunities for social improvement seen from the perspective of the protection of rights, and economic growth as there is no direct relation with FDI. It can also affect the protection of enviroment and culture as these have to give way to the economic interests of MNCs. In this way, the IIL system transforms into a type of global dictatorship in which actions against the host states with direct impact to the populations are fully legalised, controlling the social costs of independence, colonisation and to challenging the economic status quo according to which the south exists to provide raw materials for the developed world to opperate.

CONCLUSION

IIL has facilitated the economic operations of MNCs on a global scale protecting their operations, and including legitimising the plunder of resources throughout the Third World (Pahuja 2011). As a result of their economic and technological dependence, as well as the developmentalism framework, non-industrialised countries are left with fewer options when the moment comes to decide whether or not to enter into international agreements for the protection of foreign investment. This is more problematic considering that treaties for the protection of foreign investors are positioned above the polis; they protect only the rights of the investor, over the local norms and over the interests of people from the host country.

From the perspective of the Third World, the existence of an international system for the protection of foreign assets, as an alternative to domestic courts resembles the colonial past when foreigners from Western colonial powers had a special legal treatment in the colonies as well as in other independent countries subjugated by the West. As happened during the colonial times, today's alternative for the foreign investor to appear before an arbitral investment tribunal and not before domestic courts are linked to concepts of epistemological superiority and the distrust of the Orient (Said 2007).

Although, the IIL system is changing in the sense that not only are peripheral countries but also developed countries being affected by the treaties. It is therefore important not to lose sight of the fact that the whole IIL system was designed within a North-South structure. This reality, still present today, is reflected in the fact that a significantly greater number of investment claims are filed against capital importer countries by comparison with capital exporter.

Thus, the IIL system contributes in maintaining unbalanced legal, economic and political conditions, that have a direct impact on the social, psychological and phsycial integrity of citizens of non-industrialised countries. It restricts, among other things, opportunities for social improvement, economic growth, environmental protection and culture. IIL limits the ability of host peripheral countries to regulate in regards to matters of public interest whenever it affects the economic interests of foreign investors. The conclusion is that IIL is an instrument that facilitates processes of IIL systemic violence.

Today, IIL stands are guided by corporatocracy, profit and accumulation. In this sense, IIL has become an effective instrument that facilitates processes of international systemic violence. Its real aim is not the improvement of the host country, but rather the protection of the economic interests of foreign investors (Bulhan 1985). Peripheral countries have and are experiencing how their ability to intervene positively in issues of environment, health and basic facilities, among others, have been (and is) limited, affecting the interests of their own populations. In the following chapters, various elements mentioned here such as encryption and ideology will be further developed.

Chapter 2

Fault-Lines

*In-between Moving Abroad and Attracting Foreign Direct Investment**

> *The national bourgeoisie discovers its historical mission as intermediary...its vocation is not to transform the nation but prosaically serve as a conveyor belt for capitalism, forced to camouflage itself behind the mask of neocolonialism.* (Fanon 2004)

INTRODUCTION

This chapter offers an analysis from a political-economy perspective on the relationship between foreign investors and states within the framework of a global capitalist market. Hence, the chapter discusses, as part of the capitalist logic of accumulating more, the reasons for a capitalist to invest abroad. Furthermore, the chapter analyses the reasons for the Third World to seek Foreign Direct Investment (FDI), linking it to a developmentalism discourse and problematising the materialisation of the promises surrounding FDI.

In this chapter, I offer the reader a political-economy background in order to clarify the argument presented in the previous chapter according to which IIL is an instrument that facilitates systemic violence. Understanding why a company wants to invest in a country like Colombia or why a country such as Venezuela would like to attract FDI and, as such, sign International

---

* I used the concept of 'fault lines' based on the book of Hans Lindahl (see: Hans Lindahl, *Fault Lines of Globalization: Legal Order and the Politics of A-Legality* (Oxford University Press 2013). It is used in the sense of highlighting the existence of a clear and not mobile line between the reasons for Capitalists to invest abroad and the reasons for Third World Countries to attract FDI. Specifically, in the sense that, although, the lines created by the argumentative structures cannot be shifted, as the reasons are totally different, they are overstepped for the benefit of the foreign investor.

Investment Agreements (IIA), sheds light on this maze, that looks more like a mess, of the International Investment Law (IIL) system.

Capitalism and colonialism created a global economic structure characterised by an economic disparity which forced an economic division between centre and periphery at the global level (Wallerstein 2007). This division was represented in binary categories such as capital importer and capital exporter, industrialised and non-industrialised or developed and developing (Wallerstein 2007, 6–8). In this context, one of the forms of economic expansion world-wide has been the 'transfer of tangible or intangible assets from one country to another' with the aim of generating capital (Sornarajah 2010, 8). Investing abroad has served as a means to channel the possibility to appropriate the value of labour and production in the periphery so as to create more wealth, hence accumulating more capital (Appadurai 2016, 10–12).

In general terms, investments can be categorised in Foreign Portfolio Investment (FPI) and Foreign Direct Investment (FDI). FPI refers to the action when an investor moves money to purchase shares in another country or through the purchase of securities as happens primarily in Stock Exchanges and does not have a sense of permanence of time in a certain country.[2]

It is important to highlight that the IIL system has been historically more concerned in protecting FDI and not FPI. Some reasons argued for FPI not to be protected by the IIL system is that FPI usually happens in the context of Stock Exchanges using electronic procedures. It can happen in any part of the world at any time, and it is therefore difficult for the host state to be aware of the different operations which occur (Sornarajah 2010, 8–9). It is also important to highlight that FPI is under less risk of being affected by decisions adopted by a host country as investors could easily sell shares, and their operations are regulated by domestic financial law and by what can referred to as International Financial Law (IFL) (Wallace 1985).

---

[2] More specifically, Foreign Investment in general terms refers to the transferable of tangible or intangible assets from one country to another in order to generate further economic gains. the form of private economic flows. Accordingly, the two main forms of foreign investment are Foreign Direct Investment (FDI) and Foreign Portfolio Investment (FPI). FDI refers to the transference of physical elements or money from an entity in a home country to a host country in order to directly pursue an economic activity in the host country in order to increase the accumulation capacity. FDI can take the form of transfer of money to build a plant, or to purchase an already existing industry or the transfer of physical equipment among others; an important element is the intention to stay in the host country for a considerable period of time. In the case of FPI, for the movement of money from the home country to the host country in order to purchase market instruments that include shares, bond notes, and financial derivatives. This type of investment is usually done via stock exchanges and characterises for the lack of intention to stay in the host country for a considerable period of time. (see UNCTAD Secretariat, *Comprehensive Study of the Interrelationship between Foreign Direct Investment (FDI) and Foreign Portfolio Investment (FPI)* (United Nations Conference on Trade and Development 23 June 1999; Sornarajah (n 3); and Oliver de Schutter, Johan Swinnen and Jan Wouters (eds), *Foreign Direct Investment and Human Development: The Law and Economics of International Investment Agreements* (Routledge, 2013).

In the case of FDIs, this refers to the transference of physical elements to another country, and accordingly seeking economic returns with certain degree of permanence over time.[3] Accordingly, FDI can adopt one of the following forms: (i) natural resource seeking; (ii) market seeking; (iii) efficiency seeking; or (iv) strategic-asset-seeking (United Nations Conference on Trade and Development 1999; Liseth Colen 2013). As discussed in this chapter, Third World countries, have become more eager to attract FDI. This eagerness of Third World countries is the result of many different causes, including the developmentalism discourse (that constructs an aspirational context), plus the encroachment of neoliberalism as an ideology.

Accordingly, the attraction of FDI has become a constant of the legal and economic policies of Third World countries as it is expected to create job opportunities, increase national revenues and facilitate spill-overs in terms of knowledge, technology, management practices and cleaner technology in the host country (United Nations Conference on Trade and Development 1999). However, the causation between the arrival of FDI and the expectations of host Third World countries is not clear cut and, in fact, has been rather questionable.

INVESTING ABROAD

Today's global market is characterised by the easy and secure movement of capital, the use of technology to facilitate economic transactions and the existence of global commodity chains (Coronil 2000) (Piketty 2014). However, the competition proper to the capitalist system, creates an environment of constant struggle between capitalist in the global market (Dussel 2014, 145).

Capitalism promotes a constant competition for accumulation of capital that rewards the economically fittest. This competition happens in various stages: production, distribution, exchange and financial transactions (Wallerstein, Historical Capitalism with Capitalist Civilization 2011). Capitalists are always seeking to increase their shares in the global market and to reduce production, distribution and transaction costs. Hence, competition among capitalists becomes the driving force of capitalism, domestically and internationally (Chang 2014).

In this panorama of constant competition, the capitalist is forced to find new alternatives, new markets and new ways to remain competitive in the market and to continue increasing her profits. The logic that follows the capitalist system is to reward the economically fittest and to punish the

---

[3] It is important to clarify that the protection of shares is different to the protection offered to portfolio investments.

economically weakest. Accordingly, capitalists are in constant competition to be more efficient, reducing production costs, thus accumulating more profits (Chang, Economics: the User's Guide 2014).

Constant competition also forces capitalists to continually adapt to new market conditions in order not to be left behind by the system. One mode of adaptation to new market circumstances has always been to move production or certain parts of the production chain to other jurisdictions, where it is possible to access new markets and customers, to find cheaper labour, cheaper materials, more flexible legal systems or to find lower taxes, among other benefits (Wouters, Sanderijn and Hachez 2013; World Bank, 2018).

Reducing costs is a very important capitalist strategy as it allows goods and services to be offered at a price that guarantees a highest profit margin, while at the same time capturing an important chunk of the market (which is only possible by maximising the ability to produce goods at a fair price) which allows the capitalist to accumulate more and more capital (Wallerstein, Historical Capitalism with Capitalist Civilization 2011).The possibility of accumulating more capital, grants the capitalist the possibility of increased competitiveness in the global market as the surplus allows her to invest in Research and Development (R&D), to develop new procedures and technology, to improve production or to develop new products (Wallerstein, Historical Capitalism with Capitalist Civilization 2011). In this context, investing abroad is a strategy for capitalists to reduce costs and to be more competitive in the global market.

FDI can be classified by four different types depending on investors interests: (i) natural resource seeking; (ii) market seeking; (iii) efficiency seeking; and (iv) strategic-asset-seeking (United Nations Conference on Trade and Development 1999; World Bank, 2018, p. 22). In the first scenario (natural resource seeking), the investor moves to another jurisdiction in order to directly exploit raw materials that are exported without further transformation. This type of investment focuses on extractive industries such as oil, natural gas and/or mining. In the second scenario (market seeking), the investor moves to a country in order to open a new market for her product or service. Investment of this type mainly focuses on telecommunications or electricity and manufactured products.

In the third scenario (efficiency seeking), the investor settles in a Third World country which then forms a part of the production value chain in order to reduce production costs (i.e. lower wages, taxes or legal flexibility in regard to environmental or labour rights). Finally, in the fourth scenario, the investor moves to another jurisdiction to invest in R&D capabilities. However, this last type of investment is scarce in developing countries and is more focused in developed countries.

FDI can adopt the form of Greenfield investments or Merger and Acquisition investments (M&A) (Davies, et al., 2015). Greenfield is the type of investment in which the investor sets up new production facilities from the ground up, such as an industrial plant or opening a new office, among other options (Colen, Maertens y Swinnen 2013). To the contrary, M&A investment involves the acquisition of existing assets by means of a full or partial transfer of ownership or 'the merging of the capital and assets of an existing company' in the host state with another company (Colen, Maertens y Swinnen 2013; Harms & Méon, 2018, p. 38). In this case, the acquisition of a local company by a Multinational Corporation (MNC) does not necessarily mean modernisation of the technology or processes nor the creation of new jobs other than those already in place (Agosin 2010; Harms & Méon, 2018, p. 38).

For MNCs, investing abroad, to have IIL as an international legal framework for the protection of their economic activities is also an important instrument that guarantees the protection of their profits. If a regulation or a politically motivated governmental decision is adopted, then the investor can turn to an International Investment Agreement (IIA) to challenge such decisions and to seek reparation for an internationally wrongful act of the state. In this context, investing abroad with a secure legal framework makes it a worthwhile activity. That is why, and as mentioned in first chapter, MNCs used Western states to create and strengthen the legal web of international treaties in order to protect and secure their economic activity on a global scale. MNCs also use their lobbying and links (corporatocracy) in their home state to put pressure on other states to enter into international treaties that protect foreign investment (Pilkington 2016). On the other hand, MNCs put pressure on peripheral states to accept entry into IIAs as well as in allowing MNCs, acting as foreign investors, to pursue their activities in the host country.

THE THIRST FOR FDI BY THIRD WORLD COUNTRIES

During the colonial period, the metropolis controlled the economic policies of its colonies. Hence, colonies did not have a broad chance of deciding whether to allow foreigners to enter their markets or to make profits by setting up enterprises within the colonies (either to plunder local natural resources or to reduce production costs by using free labour from the host colonies). After the nineteenth and twentieth centuries decolonisation processes, former colonies became independent countries and were immediately incorporated into the global capitalist economy. The incorporation process was formally portrayed as the welcoming of new actors, when in reality, the newly independent countries had always been a part of the global dynamic.

Nonetheless, the economic dependence created under the colonial economic structure, was maintained and continued throughout and within the post-colonial setting. Hence, newly independent countries, although politically sovereign and independent, continued to be economically and technologically dependent on former colonial centres (F. Fanon 2004). This reality forced Third World countries to allow foreigners to continue plundering their natural resources and to continue exploiting their citizens. Capitalists from Western Europe and North America took over former colonies through MNCs such as the United Fruit Company or via mining companies operating mines in Rhodesia (now Zimbabwe). Fanon clearly described this disadvantageous situation manifest in the relationship between the Third World and foreign private capital:

> It is a fact that young nations attract little private capital. A number of reasons justify and explain these reservations on the part of the monopolies. As soon as the capitalist know, and they are obviously the first to know, that their government is preparing to decoloni[s]e, they hasten to withdraw all their capital from the colony. This spectacular flight of capital is one of the most constant phenomena of decoloni[s]ation. In order to invest in the independent countries, private companies demand terms which from experience prove unacceptable or unfeasible. (Fanon 2004, 59)

The developmentalism discourse also played an important role reinforcing the need to attract foreign capital as it was perceived as an important element to reach the land of milk and honey of development. The developmentalism discourse changed the political discourse of barbarism and civilisation into the economic discourse of development and coined the term 'economic backwardness'.

After the Second World War, the semantics of 'backwardness' and 'uncivilised' were transformed into the economic semantic of 'developed' and 'developing' and by, association carrying an implication of an aspect of social progress. Truman's discourse marked what scholars refer as the century of development, continuing with the world division into categories where the periphery (the other) continued occupying a backwards position when compared with the West (Baxi 2009, 94).

It is important to remember that in the aftermath of the Second World War, on 20 January 1949, U.S. President Harry S. Truman delivered a speech in which he brought into international politics and international relations, the term 'underdevelopment', referring to economic backwardness; the fourth point of Truman's speech stated the following:

> Fourth, we must embark on a bold new program for making the benefits of our scientific advances and industrial progress available for the improvement and growth of underdeveloped areas. (Truman 1949)

Development was understood as uni-lineal stages of change in which peripheral societies were behind, in a sort of adolescent stage, not able to stand up to modern developments and in need of adult guidance – a role adopted by Western countries (Rist 2008, 61). In this form, Truman's speech marked the new Manichean division of the world into developed and underdeveloped (no longer colonised or coloniser) making it clear that it was the developed countries that would decide the future of the world. For the first time, a society could accelerate along the path of history in order to reach a stage of development, following 'scientific programs' (created by the West, which would modify law, local economic structures, cultures, among others) (Pahuja 2011, 62).

According to this logic, the other continued being the 'wretched of the earth', those that in Hobbesian terms live in a state of nature, with hunger, illnesses, poverty and corruption (Baxi 2009). Underdevelopment was assumed to be the result of a natural occurrence, unrelated to past violent acts, such as colonisation. In this regard, Gilbert Rist states the following:

> Development took on a transitive meaning (an action performed by one agent upon another) which corresponded to a principle of social organization, while underdevelopment became a naturally occurring (that is, seemingly causeless) state of things. (Rist 2008, 73)

Development efforts were presented as international attempts to overcome the existing socio-economic gap between developed and developing countries (Wallerstein, 1993). Development was assumed by the West as a goal to be universally shared by all the people of the world, including the worst off (Baxi 2009).

The idea that development would occur in a market-friendly environment fuelled by the need for foreign investment. In this context, FDI was portrayed as an element essential for a developing country in order to reach the goal of 'development'. FDI was expected to create job opportunities, increase national revenues and to facilitate spill-overs in the areas of knowledge, technology, management practices and cleaner technology in the host country.

The Partnership for Growth and Development during the Ninth UN Conference on Trade and Development discussed the existing link between development and FDI in the following terms:

> [F]oreign direct investment (FDI) can play a key role in the economic growth and development process. The importance of FDI for development has dramatically increased in recent years. FDI is now considered to be an instrument through which economies are being integrated at the level of production into the globalising world economy by bringing a package of assets, including capital, technology, managerial capacities and skills, and access to foreign markets. It also stimulates technological capacity-building for production, innovation

and entrepreneurship within the larger domestic economy through catalysing backward and forward linkages. (United Nations Conference on Trade and Development 1999)

It was argued that companies acting as domestic suppliers for the foreign investor could benefit through know-how and technological spill-overs. It was expected that a domestic firm, working for the foreign investor, would need to adapt to the standards required by the foreign investor which standards would usually be, according to the literature, higher and more efficient than those of domestic companies (Colen, Maertens y Swinnen 2013).

Other forms of spill-overs to local companies would happen by way of transmission of know-how through the hiring of host country workers. It was argued that when a worker, who had previously worked for a foreign investor was then hired by a local company, that worker could share the knowledge and skills acquired with the local company (it was expected and presumed that the worker's skills and knowledge would improve during the time working with the foreign investor).

It was also argued that domestic companies could also benefit from spill-overs through the process of reverse engineering. Reverse engineering is the process by which a company legally unpacks the manufacturing process of a certain good or a service provided and tries to imitate it (Colen, Maertens y Swinnen 2013). Following the reverse engineering process, it was expected that the local firm would improve its know-how, technology and corporate practices.

Other arguments, about the benefits of FDI and its contribution to the development of the local economy are linked to the existing technological gap between capital-importing and capital-exporting countries. On the one hand, it was argued that foreign investment is needed as there are activities that are very unlikely to be performed or products be manufactured by domestic firms as a result of the technological gap as well as by the limitations derived from the existence of intellectual property rights.

On the other hand, it was also argued that although it may be possible for domestic companies to perform certain activities or to manufacture certain goods, this would only happen in the long term (Agosin 2010). Thus, the foreign investor enters to fill the gap left in the internal market caused by technological backwardness, which local market would avoid having to wait a long time for domestic firms to provide the service or manufacture the goods.

Following the same logic, it was expected that the local economy could benefit from foreign investment arriving in the country as competition created by foreign actors would force domestic companies to invest in Research and Development (R&D) in order to stay afloat in the market. Investment in R&D

pursued by domestic companies would create benefits for local know-how, industry and for the country as a whole (Agosin 2010; World Bank 2018; pp. 116, 117; AlAzzawi 2012; Tan & Azman-Saini 2017; Lu, et al. 2017, p. 88). Finally, among the long list of FDI benefits, it is argued that FDI contributes to the relief from poverty through the creation of employment, by revenues left in the host country, by wage improvement and by the growth of the local economy in general (Colen, Maertens y Swinnen 2013).

Considering the long list of benefits drawn to peripheral countries by FDI, Third World countries began a race to attract foreign investment. The interest to attract more foreign investment to peripheral countries, became a central part of the agenda of Third World countries from the late 1970s onwards, coinciding with the rise of neoliberalism as the new hegemonic ideology. Data shows that since 1980 the share of global FDI inflows to developing countries increased from 14 per cent in 1980 to 30 per cent by 2006 (Colen, Maertens y Swinnen 2013) and up to 44.5 per cent in 2020 (United Nations Conference on Trade and Development, 2020, p. 13).

Different mechanisms were put in place by capital-importer countries to attract more FDI, including adapting domestic law to fulfill the interests of foreign investors (Perry-Kessaris 2008). Nonetheless, the foremost important factor was the signing of Bilateral Investment Treaties (BITs) with capital-exporter countries in order to become more attractive to foreign investors (Saad-Filho 2005). BITs were used as instruments to send signals to the business community by capital-importing countries (Dolzer y Stewvens 1995, 12; Kerner 2009, pp. 78–82; Dixon & Haslam 2016, pp. 1080, 1083). The competition to attract FDI to their territory simultaneously deepened the divisions among Third World countries,[4] resembling the old colonial practice pursued by the colonial powers of dividing colonised continents for the benefit of the colonisers (Fanon 2004). This vigorous competition made capital-importer countries accept stronger clauses in treaties signed with capital-exporter countries in such terms that the sovereignty of the host state in matters of public interest was put in jeopardy (Wouters, Sanderijn, & Hachez 2013).

In this context, Third World countries got caught in a competition amongst each other, to become active players of the global market and to receive an important share of FDI in their territory. This race between Third World countries, encouraged by a developmentalism discourse and a neoliberal ideology, materialised in what Fanon refers to as oppressors

---

[4] One example is the case of the FTA negotiated between Peru, Colombia, and the European Union. Colombia and Peru decided to separate themselves from the other countries aiming at winning the race of investment attraction. For more information see European Commission, 'Andean Community' Countries and Regions <http://ec.europa.eu/trade/policy/countries-and-regions/regions/andean-community/> accessed 2 January 2017.

employing every opportunity to put the 'other' to fight each against the other (Fanon 2004, 87).

SHADOWS OF ILLUSIONS

The apparent benefits brought by FDI and BITs to Third World countries have fallen under constant scrutiny and have been criticised from different standpoints by academics, politicians, social movements, activists and others. Beginning with BITs, empirical literature is divided between studies that show that signing BITs increases the influx of FDI to host countries (Hallward-Driemeier 2009, 349; Egger y Merlo 2007; Neumayer y Spess 2005; Salacuse y Sullivan 2009, 109; Lejour & Salfi, 2014, pp. 28–29; Bhasin & Manocha, 2016, p. 285) while other empirical studies have reached a different conclusion. For instance, a UN study found no relation between BITs and inflows of FDI. The study concluded that BITs play a secondary role in attracting FDI to a country (United Nations Conference on Trade and Development 2007). Likewise, other studies have pointed out the absence of a strong impact of BITs on FDI inflows for developing countries by comparison to developed countries (Min, et al. 2011, p. 75; Yackee, 2011).

Furthermore, a study of the Columbia Centre on Sustainable Investment pointed out some of the advantages and costs of investment treaties. Regarding the expected benefits, the researchers established that some of these included an 'increased inward investment, [an] increased outward investment and [the] depoliticization of disputes'. On the other hand, some of the costs noted comprised of the 'reputational cost, reduced policy space, distorted power dynamics, reduced role for domestic law-making, uncertainty in law' (Johnson, 2018, p.3).

Some of the reasons for the division among empirical studies into the relationship between BITs and FDI relates to differences in research methods, sectors and/or the scope of the research. However, the simple fact that there is no unanimity as to whether BITs attract FDI to a host country must be considered as a red flag for a Third World country about the benefits of and the need to sign this type of treaty.

An analogous situation occurs with the benefits created by FDI in the economy of a host country. One important criticism of FDI has to do with the fact that an important influx of foreign investment in certain sectors of the economy can create a 'crowding-out' (CO) effect. The CO effect refers to ta situation in which foreign investors displace domestic firms that otherwise would have invested in the development activity of manufacturing certain goods in the absence of the Foreign Investors (Szkorupova 2015; Göçer, Mercan y Peker 2014; Agosin, y otros 2000; Jude 2018; Morrissey & Udomkerdmongkol 2012; Brennan & Ruane 2016).

Also, receiving FDI in specific domestic industries pre-empts future opportunities for domestic companies to participate in the market, to create and to innovate (Agosin 2010, p. 23; Morrissey & Udomkerdmongkol 2012, p. 443). Another important criticism is the fact that when FDI enters an economic sector in which there were previously domestic firms producing either for the domestic market or for export, it is likely that FDI might pre-empt investment opportunities (Agosin, 2010, p. 23). The foreign investor's technological superiority, 'infrastructural capacity, skill base, cluster strengths and supply chain networks' (Matthew et al. 2018, p. 17) aggregated to domestic factors such as the difficulty of local firms competing with foreign investors' financial muscle (as it is even difficult to borrow from local banks) creates a situation where local companies are undoubtedly displaced by the foreign investor.

Regarding job creation, FDI does not guarantee the creation of new positions for local workers. Greenfield investments clearly generate jobs in the local economy, but it is not the case with Mergers and Acquisitions (M&A) investments (Greenfield and M&A investments were explained earlier in this chapter). For instance, in India, FDI has been less than expected and investment fell more into the form of Mergers & Acquisitions than in the form of Greenfield Investments that operate more as new enterprise which is considered to have a more positive impact on the local economy (Perry-Kessaris 2008).

The impact on employment of M&A and privatisations is mixed, while the impact of Greenfield investment is high (Economic Commission for Latin America and the Caribbean (ECLAC), 2013, p. 108). M&A investments are a very popular form of FDI in Third World countries as result of privatisation processes of publically owned companies or the purchase of domestic industries by big foreign multinationals.

Whenever there is an M&A investment, job creation is uncertain as the investor takes over an already existing company, and likely maintains the number of workers. In seeking to increase profitability of the new acquisition, it is also likely to render a certain number of workers redundant. It is also important to consider that in terms of M&A investments, it is very unlikely that a foreign investor will bring in new technology, especially if the company taken over has done well economically during the years prior to the M&A acquisition.

In terms of developing countries' economic growth, the relationship between FDI, economic growth and improvement in the economic and social conditions of the entire population of the host country are also unclear. The economic growth of a country is usually measured by the Gross Domestic Product (GDP) a monetary measure of all the goods and services produced in country in the period of a quarter of a year or one year (Piketty 2014, 43). In this sense although the arrival of FDI to a Third World country could be positively reflected in its GDP, it does not necessarily mean that the improvement in figures materialises to the benefit of the whole of society (Piketty 2014). In specific industries such as those related with hydrocarbons, the economic benefit is received by a small portion of society as taxes or royalties paid (aimed at expanding the benefit to the whole of society) are low. In fact, among other challenges arising out of FDI's arrival is how to avoid a concentration of economic power and income in the upper layers of society (Guardiola-Rivera 2013, pp. 44–45).

Another important economic criticism related to FDI has to do with the final destination of profits made by the foreign investor as they are usually sent abroad. An important influx of domestic money is sent to the MNC's home country affecting the economy of host country and is reflected in the national income rate (Piketty 2014). Regardless that many profits end up passing through tax havens to avoid taxation either in the host state or the home state, the money earned as profits by foreign investors tends to end up in central economies (directly or indirectly) via shareholders, reflecting a geographical flow from the periphery to the centre in the global economy (Swamy 2011) (Anderson 2014; Briseño Perezyera et al., 2015).

Neither is there clarity about the benefits of the transfer of knowledge and technology in the form of spill-lovers. Regarding spill-overs for domestic companies, it is insufficiently clear how, for instance, reverse engineering would allow domestic companies to improve their processes if there are legal barriers that impede such transfers, and referring specifically to all the intellectual property norms at the domestic and international levels. In terms of transference of know-how to local employees, the benefits are also unclear, leaving many doubts. The main doubt arises out of the way in which companies work within the capitalist system in the sense of maintaining competitiveness in the global market in order to continue accumulating profits.

In this sense, there are no economic incentives for a foreign investor to focus on fully promoting the technology or know-how transfer to local companies or local employees, as it could make local companies competitive and consequently affect the foreign investor's competitive advantage in the market. In this context, foreign investors adopt specific legal measures such as confidentiality agreements to maintain secrecy of formulas or procedures (i.e. trade secrets) to protect their competitive advantage. This translates into protecting their investment returns and therefore allowing an accumulation of capital (Colen & Guariso 2013).

Considering all the existing criticisms towards the real benefits of FDI and the IIL system, it is relevant to explore cases of countries that have adopted other approaches towards FDI and IIL to overcome some of the aforementioned criticisms. For instance, countries such as China or Taiwan are characterised by their adoption of unorthodox policies towards foreign investment entering their markets including the imposition of strict controls on foreign investments (Piketty 2014, 71). In the case of China, for a foreigner to invest in a Chinese firm, government authorisation is required (Piketty 2014). Another interesting aspect of Chinese control of foreign investment is the strong limitations on M&A investments as a means of discouraging those operations; indeed, making them almost non-existent (Agosin, Is Foreign Investment Always Good for Development? 2010, 26). Moreover, despite existing controls and strong restrictions on foreign investment, economically, China has performed very well in the global market. In fact, a recent study showed that the restrictions on short-term capital inflows can improve FDI inflows as they can be perceived as a sign of stability (Nugent III 2019).

Another example is the Republic of Taiwan that imposed a prohibition (which lasted until 1990) on each foreign investor not owning more than 15 per cent of a domestic company (Agosin, Is Foreign Investment Always Good for Development? 2010). The regulation also foreign ownership of a national company exceeding 30 per cent (Agosin, Is Foreign Investment Always Good for Development? 2010). The policy of the Taiwanese government attempted to discourage M&A foreign investment which, as discussed earlier, does not bring much benefit to the host economy. Even though the regulation lasted only until the 1990s, it turned out well economically for the success of the Taiwanese economy.

The case of Singapore is also interesting not only because almost all land is owned by the government (no particulars available or provided) but because they promote state-owned enterprises, which produce almost 22 per cent of national output. This places less importance on promoting and encouraging FDI (Chang, Economics: the User's Guide 2014). Of course, the foregoing is not necessarily to say that those are the policies to follow, but rather to highlight that there are alternatives in the form of how to regulate FDI in a host country in order to really secure a win-win situation between the foreign investor and the host country.

CONCLUSION

The current global market and global economic divisions between developed and developing countries is based on inequalities originating in the colonial structure. Furthermore, the ability of capitalist investors from the metropolis to mobilise around the world to reduce costs, source new raw materials, find lower wage structures (or not pay wages at all) or to open up new markets, has existed since colonial times.

The only difference is that technology has facilitated material and/or financial movement around the world. In the current global market, the commodity chain has followed a pattern where the origins tend to be located all around the world, but the final destination is a reduced, very diffused physical and social area.

In the constant competition for more accumulation, capitalists have tried to reduce production costs by moving abroad in order to obtain lower priced raw materials as well as lower labour costs. In this context, the capitalist system has forced peripheral countries to specialise in the exploitation of raw materials and cheap labour.

The specialisation of capital importer countries as places for the exploitation of raw materials and cheap labour has affected their economic fitness, in an economic system that rewards the economically strongest by making them less competitive in the global market. In this scenario, developing countries are not only opening their domestic markets to foreign investors but are handing over their natural and human resources without clarity about the economic benefits that will be received by them.

Furthermore, the developmentalism discourse, which promises happiness (by reaching the promised land of development), has managed to disguise patterns of unequal distribution and the plunder of peripheral countries as enhanced by FDI and its international legal regulation (IIL system). Developing countries are focused on the aspirational dream of becoming developed countries. This logic of modernisation and economic advancement behind the developmentalism discourse has been the framework for the promotion of an environment favourable to foreign investors because FDI has been portrayed as essential for a country to reach their developmental aspirations.

Linking foreign investment and development kicked off a race to the bottom amongst developing countries to attract foreign investment. They entered into more BITs and FTAs, while adopting regulations favourable to MNCs in order to become more attractive to foreign investors. This competition simultaneously deepened the divisions among Third World countries, thus resembling the old colonial practice of dividing colonised continents for the benefit of the colonisers.

In this context, the IIL system appeared as an international legal structure to protect private property and the ability to accumulate capital in the international market. In this way, the IIL system is directly rooted in capitalist dynamics of accumulation of profit and relations of production offering enhanced legal protection to forms of relations of capitalist exploitation, aimed at accumulating surplus.

Accordingly, it is important not to lose sight of the fact that despite IIL having a global materialisation, it is a system that has originated within the North-South structure. In conclusion, it is not possible to understand the IIL system without seeing it as an instrument for the protection of the capitalist system and as a result of colonial relationships.

Chapter 3

The Riddle of Treaties and Awards

> *In any case it would come up against the implacable opposition of the former metropolis, which will have taken every possible precaution in the framework of neo-colonialist agreements.* (F. Fanon 2004, 123)

INTRODUCTION

In the previous chapter, I offered an analysis of how and why Foreign Direct Investment (FDI) flows to developing countries, and why it has been presented as a *sine qua non* element in order to reach the promised land of development. Along this same line, I offered the reader in chapter 1 an analysis of the two main elements of the International Investment Law (IIL) system: (i) International Investment Agreements (IIA) and (ii) the Investor State Dispute Settlement (ISDS) system. In this chapter I intend to offer the appropriate groundwork to the specialised and the non-specialised reader to further build the argument that IIL facilitates systemic violence.

Before the end of the Second World War, foreign property was protected either via gunboat diplomacy or diplomatic protection (Hathaway and Shapiro 2017; Piketty 2014). In both cases, the home state directly assumed the protection of the economic interests of the foreign investor before the host state, seeking the withdrawal of measures or the payment of compensation according to 'international standards', that is Western standards. Notorious cases of gunboat diplomacy for the protection of private property include the opium war between Britain and China and the Nanking Treaty of 1842, or the 1092–1903 attack on Caracas by German, British and Italian warships. In both situations, Western military capabilities allowed the enforcement and protection of the rights of private property and economic interests (Chang, Economics: the User's Guide 2014).

With the formal end of colonisation, newly independent countries pursued domestic and international policies seeking to redress unfair economic injustices that had happened during colonial and imperial times, thus challenging the status quo. In this context, decolonisation and the two World Wars meant a reduction of Western assets abroad, consequently threatening the economic advantages and welfare of the West (Piketty 2014, 121).

In this international environment, international law was adapted as an instrument that also served, among different objectives, to protect foreign owned property in the Third World. Specifically, International Investment Law (IIL) consolidated as a system to regulate relations between host states and foreign investors having as a relevant aim the protection of property and investments in general. This system also standardised what is to be considered legal and illegal towards the foreign investor on a global scale, imposing a Western point of view onto the rest of the world.

IIA, specifically Bilateral Investment Treaties (BITs), were 'agreed' between former colonialist centres and peripheral countries.[1] These treaties protect investments, including the protection of physical assets, intellectual rights, administrative rights and shareholder's rights. From the very beginning, IIA (including BITs and later investment chapters within Free Trade Agreements FTAs) were characterised as being treaties of adhesion, as peripheral countries had little bargaining power in 'take it or leave it' treaties.

THE TREATIES

The first modern BIT was signed in 1959 between the Republic of Germany and Pakistan (Treaty for the Promotion and Protection of Investments (with Protocol and exchange of notes) Pakistan and Federal Republic of Germany 1959). The German government at the time was concerned with the risks of losing more investments abroad, especially considering that they had already lost an important part of their foreign investments abroad following

---

[1] The reference in inverted commas of the word 'agreed' connoting an ironic use of the term, is done in order to make the reader aware that although the treaties are presented as bilaterally negotiated between two equal and sovereign countries, the reality is different. As, briefly mentioned in the introduction of this book and as part of the argumentative line presented throughout all the chapters of this book, BITs and FTA in regards to Third World counties are the result of historic events that include the epistemic and economic superiority of central countries compared to Third World countries and the hegemonic positioning of neoliberalism as ideology at the heart of a capitalist economic system.

the country's defeat in the Second World War (Neumann, Marcuse, and Kirchheimer 2013).

Subsequent to this first treaty, BITs have undergone different modifications and innovations over time. However, from the very beginning, these treaties have been characterised as being standardised agreements featuring similar principles and clauses world-wide.

The common principles and clauses featured in BITs include the definition of investment and investor and anti-discriminatory measures – National Treatment and Most Favoured Nation (MFN). They also include Fair and Equitable Treatment (FET), protection against expropriation (direct and indirect), security clauses and dispute settlement mechanisms. As we move forward, this chapter will briefly touch upon some of those clauses which are considered the most relevant in BITs world-wide.

The definitions of 'investor' and 'investment' are both constructed upon the description of capitalist activities pursued by the movement of capital abroad in order to accumulate greater profits. The term 'investors' in IIAs includes natural and legal persons from both contracting parties. In the case of legal persons, and in order to determine the nationality of the foreign investor, some IIAs include different nationality tests, such as the seat of control or where there is substantial interest or certain level of control, or the test of incorporation and control (Sornarajah 2010, 198–199). IIAs also offer protection to subsidiaries of companies when they are wholly or majority-owned by foreign investors, although this protection has also been extended to minority shareholders (Gaukrodger 2014).

Investment, for the purposes of BITs, refers to the 'transfer of tangible or intangible assets from one country to another' with the aim of generating capital (Sornarajah 2010, 8). As mentioned in chapter 2, foreign investments can be either Portfolio or Foreign Direct Investments. Foreign Portfolio Investment (FPI) refers to the action when an investor using stock exchanges purchases securities with no intention of future long-lasting permanence (Sornarajah 2010). Foreign Direct Investment (FDI) relates to the transfer of physical elements or financial resources to another country with an aim of permanence in time. IIA have historically focused on the protection of FDI.[2] However, in more recent years, some IIA have extended the protection to FPI (Sornarajah 2010, 196–197).

The development of the investment clause has passed through different stages. BITs began with the protection of foreign-owned property and passed through various stages until reaching the point of including the treaty's

---

[2] It is important to clarify that the protection of shares is different to the protection offered to portfolio investments.

wording of the term 'investment'. The term 'investment' has a wider scope and implies duration and movement (Yannaca-Small and Liberti 2008).

Initially treaties offered protection only to property owned by foreigners, and it was expected that host states would have to guarantee minimum standards to the physical property owned by the foreigner. After the decision of the International Court of Justice (ICJ) in the Barcelona Traction Case, shares, were also included in the definition of investment in BITs.[3] The next big incorporation in the scope of the investment within BITs was the protection of intellectual rights and later of administrative rights. Administrative rights refer to licences issued by administrative agencies such as environmental licences, which are essential for the foreign investor to pursue its economic activity (Sornarajah 2010).

The next common principle among BITs is the principle of non-discrimination materialised in the clauses of Most Favoured Nation (MFN) and National Treatment. These two principles have formed part of international trade relations for many years and have become an essential foundation in modern international economic law, especially in international trade and foreign investment regulation (Sornarajah 2010, 14–15). The principles of MFN and National Treatment are explained in more detail in the lines that follow.

MFN treatment means that an 'investor from a party to an agreement, or its investment, would be treated by the other party "no less favourably" with respect to a given subject matter than an investor from any third country, or its investment' (OECD 2004). The MFN principle has long formed part of the relations between European countries. During the seventeenth century, European countries included a sort of MFN clause in most bilateral treaties (Caplin y Krishna 1998). For instance, the 1692 treaty between Denmark and the Hanseatic Cities included a form of MFN clause (Caplin y Krishna 1998, 267). Friendship Commerce and Navigation (FCN) agreements also included MFN-type clauses as was the case, for example in the 1778 FCN agreement between France and the USA (OECD 2004).

National Treatment protects the rights of the investor to be treated in the same manner as the host country treats its own domestic investors without any form of discrimination. While the application of this clause may seem easy and straight-forward; however, it requires that the investments to be similar.

The Fair and Equitable Treatment (FET) principle is also important and common among IIA. It is crucial to note that, after the end of the Second World War, the USA's FCN began to include the words 'equitable' and 'fair and

---

[3] In the *Barcelona Traction* Case, the ICJ held that shares in a company that was the vehicle of foreign investment could not be protected using diplomatic protection of the shareholder's state; it was a right reserved to the state where the company was incorporated. See *Case Concerning the Barcelona Traction*, (*Belgium v Spain*) (Judgment) [1970] I.C.J. Rep 3.

equitable treatment' (OECD 2004). FET was incorporated in the 1948 Havana Charter that sought to create the International Trade Organisation (United Nations Conference on Trade and Employment 1948). FET was also included in the text of the Economic Agreement of Bogotá that was agreed upon during the Ninth International Conference of American States in Bogotá (Ninth International Conference of American States 1948). Beyond indirect expropriation, FET has become an important element at the forefront of claims filed by foreign investors against host states (Schill, Fair and Equitable Treatment under Investment Treaties as an Embodiment of the Rule of Law 2006).

Investment Arbitral Tribunals have been charged with interpreting FET and its scope of application by approaching it in different manners. Nonetheless, new IIAs tend to include a list of situations that are considered to breach this standard of treatment. The approach taken by Arbitral Tribunals regarding breaches to the FET standard has included actions such as the lack of transparency towards the foreign investor, lack of stability or consistency of the host state's legal framework, violation of due process, proportionality or violation of legitimate expectations (Metalclad Corporation v The United Mexican States 2000).

In the case of 'legitimate expectations', this has been interpreted as the protection of normative, political and economic expectations that a foreign investor has at the moment of entering/investing in the host country, and which played an essential role in the decision to invest in that specific country (Miles, The Origins of International Investment Law: Empire, Environment and The Safeguard of Capital 2015). The reasoning behind protecting legitimate expectations is the importance of creating a stable atmosphere for investors and the market, by balancing domestic regulation, norms and policies against the expectations of the foreign investor (Schill, Fair and Equitable Treatment under Investment Treaties as an Embodiment of the Rule of Law 2006).

Another important part of IIAs is the 'umbrella clause' which grants special protection to agreements signed between the host state and the investor. In that form, even if the IIA is not directly breached, the breach of a contract allows the foreign investor to rely on the BIT, including the use of ISDS, to seek redress for the breach of a contract. It is important to highlight that 'umbrella clauses' are not necessarily titled within the IIA as 'umbrella clauses' and their wording is usually similar to the following: 'Each Contracting Party shall observe any obligation it may have entered into with regard to investments of investors of the Other Contracting Party' (Agreement between the UK and Argentina for the promotion and protection of investments 1993).

The 'umbrella clause' elevates contracts between states and foreign investors to a level of quasi-treaties regulated by a special international law and by the principles of international law (Anghie 2007). Moreover, the protection offered by the umbrella clause has been approached in diverse ways by arbitral tribunals. On the one hand, umbrella clauses have been interpreted broadly by some tribunals by offering investors extensive protection of their rights while, on the other hand, different tribunals have taken a restrictive approach in interpreting such clauses (Schill, Umbrella Clauses as Public Law Concepts in Comparative Perspective 2010).

Another relevant clause that forms part of most of IIAs is the 'full protection and security clause'. This clause requires the host state to not interfere with the investor's economic activity. It also requires the host state to protect the foreign investor using coercive measures such as using the Army or the Police against harm that could be caused by third parties either as result of complicity or failure to act (Zeitler 2010).

Finally, another important aspect and common to many IIAs are those clauses related to direct and indirect expropriation. Considering the history and the origins of the IIL as a structure for the protection of foreign-owned property, the following section analyses in greater detail the protection against direct and indirect expropriation. However, for now, it is sufficient to say that IIAs protect the foreign investor against direct and indirect expropriation and the analysis of what constitutes an investment has been approached in a multiplicity of ways by investment arbitral tribunals.

DIRECT AND INDIRECT EXPROPRIATION

Private property is not only one of the essential elements of the capitalist system (as it allows accumulation) it is also at the heart of the IIL system. Crucially, the Western conception of private property was expanded not only through commercial relations but also through imperialism and colonialism. The right to private property is a subjective right with permanence throughout over time that allows its title holder to use and consume certain goods while granting a right to exclude others (*erga omnes*) (Dussel 2014, 77). Private property has been approached from different angles, including as a civil liberty that grants freedom (for instance Hayek) or as a natural right (for instance John Locke or Richard Epstein).

Furthermore, it has been argued that the state exists to protect the liberties and the right to private property of its nationals. Hence, the state should refrain from intervening or affecting that right in any way (Epstein 1985). In this regard, John Locke states the following:

> The supreme power cannot take away from any man any part of his property without his own consent. For the preservation of property being the end of the

government and that for which men entered into society, it necessarily supposes and requires that the people should have property, without which they supposed to lose that by entering into society, which was the end for which they entered into it, too gross and absurdity for any man to own. (Locke 1690)

Under this logic, private property had to be protected not only domestically but also abroad, especially in the global periphery. This interest to protect private property has been constant during different historical periods.

During the colonial and imperial period, protection of private property at the periphery was enforced directly by colonial authority. In the case of relations with the periphery that were not directly under colonial or imperial rule, gunboat diplomacy was used to protect foreign-owned property.

After decolonisation, the use of bilateral treaties was the starting point for the consolidation of an international legal system for the protection of foreign-owned property, later expanded to protect not only property but foreign investment in general. In this form, the IIL system consolidated as a legal system that offered a special protection to the foreign investor against direct and indirect expropriation.

Direct expropriation implies a direct taking of the private property by the host government, that is to remove an object from the possession of its owner or to take away the ownership title and transferring it to the host state (Epstein 1985, 38) (OECD 2004). It is argued, that when a host government pursues a direct expropriation, the host government is not only taking over the physical assets, but it is also appropriating the profits of the expropriated company, somehow generating an increase in public wealth (OECD 2004).

The traditional conception of expropriation was expanded in the 1990s to also protect the foreign investor against any form of interference that could affect the owner's ability to use or enjoy the property, including the expected profits. Accordingly, indirect expropriation refers to situations where although the owner continues owning the assets and the title over the property, it cannot continue with the economic activity, as expected, because of a measure adopted by the host state (Christie 1962; Epstein 1985).

The North American Free Trade Agreement (NAFTA) was the first major multilateral agreement to include a protection against indirect expropriation. Article 1110 of NAFTA states the following about direct and indirect expropriation:

No Party may directly or indirectly nationalise or expropriate an investment of an investor of another Party in its territory or take a measure tantamount to nationalisation or expropriation of such an investment, except:
(a) for a public purpose;
(b) on a non-discriminatory basis;

(c) in accordance with due process of law and Article 1105 (1)15 and
(d) on payment of compensation in accordance with [subsequent paragraphs specifying valuation of expropriations and form and procedure of payment].

The measure affecting the foreign investor's property can come from any public authority (judicial, executive or legislative branch) and at any level (MPs, Mayors, higher or lower courts' judges). This type of expropriation is also known as creeping, de facto expropriation or measures 'tantamount' to expropriation.

It is important to indicate at this point that Customary International Law allows host states to expropriate foreign investments whenever such expropriation complies with certain conditions. The most important condition to fulfil is to pursue the expropriation for reasons of public interest. Other conditions that must be fulfilled include following a due process that expropriation must be non-discriminatory and the state must pay a fair compensation to the expropriated party (OECD 2004).

Article 3 of the 1967 OECD Draft Convention on Foreign Property described the abovementioned requirements whenever an expropriation takes place. Specifically, Article 3 mentions the following:

Article 3: TAKING OF PROPERTY: No Party shall take any measures, directly or indirectly, of his property a national of another Party unless the following are complied with:
(i) The measures are taken in the public interest and under due process of law;
(ii) The measures are not discriminatory or contrary to any undertaking which the former Party may have given; and
(iii) The measures are accompanied by provision for the payment of just compensations. Such compensations shall represent the genuine value of the property affected, shall be paid without undue delay, and shall be transferable to the extent necessary to make it effective for the national entitled thereto. (OECD 1967)

Likewise, the 1992 Investment Guidelines issued by the World Bank stated the following regarding expropriation:

A state may not expropriate or otherwise take in whole or in part a foreign private investment in its territory, or take measures which have similar effects, except where this is done in accordance with applicable legal procedures, in pursuance in good faith of a public purpose, without discrimination on the basis of nationality and against the payment of appropriate compensation. (The World Bank Group 1992)

A similar approach was adopted by Article 13 of the 1994 Energy Charter. Article 13 establishes the prohibition of expropriation or any equivalent measure, except when such expropriation complies with the rules of customary international law, specifically the rules on public purpose, due process, non-discrimination and compensation.

The extent to what is, or what is or not considered as an interference with property is something that has been decided on a case by case basis by Investment Arbitral Tribunals and has been approached in different ways. For instance, in the case of *Santa Elena v. Costa Rica*, the tribunal held that although measures adopted by the country were for the benefit of the environment and of the society as a whole, it amounted to an indirect expropriation. The Tribunal specifically clarified that an indirect expropriation can happen, although the aims and intentions are socially acceptable or protected by other norms of international law (Compañía del Desarrollo de Santa Elena S.A. v Republic of Costa Rica 2000).

In this way, any regulation pursued by the host state could be considered as amounting to indirect expropriation, thus allowing MNCs to challenge any national or local law related to public welfare, human rights or economic regulation whenever it affects the company's investment in a host country (Greider 2001). This lack of clarity, which is a proper quality of an encrypted discourse (the topic of encryption is dealt with in more detail in the next section) creates unjustified burdens upon host countries.

As described in this section, protection against expropriation guarantees to a capitalist that whenever his assets and surplus are transferred from the private realm to the public realm, compensation must be paid for the economic loss (Epstein 1985, 168). However, such an enhanced protection based upon neoliberal principles clashes with, among others, notions of the rule of law, human rights, people's rights and environmental rights (Epstein 1985).

INVESTOR-STATE DISPUTE SETTLEMENT – ISDS

The settlement of disputes derived from conflicts between investors and host states is mainly conducted via arbitration. Investment treaties expressly delegate to investment arbitral tribunals the jurisdiction to interpret and apply the text of a treaty in order to resolve existing conflicts between investors and host states. In this context, BITs offer the investor different arbitration options which are mainly institutional or *ad hoc* arbitration. Arbitration materialises in allowing the foreign investor to seek the resolution of the conflict by an offshore non-permanent tribunal, and not exhausting domestic courts. In this form, states give up part of the sovereign control and bind themselves to submitting any dispute with the investor to an offshore arbitral tribunal

(Colen and Guariso 2013). It is important to point out that modern forms of arbitration within the context of Public International Law were mainly developed as an alternative means of resolving disputes among states. Hence, the novelty of investment arbitration as it currently operates is the possibility that an individual may file a claim against a state before a non-permanent court for economic reasons without even exhausting domestic courts.

Some early antecedents in the development of modern forms of inter-state arbitration include the Jay Treaty of 1794 (a form of FCN treaty), the treaty of Guadalupe Hidalgo in 1848 (during the Mexican War), the First Hague Conference of 1899 that founded the Permanent Court of Arbitration, and the inclusion of arbitration as dispute settlement mechanisms in BITs and FTAs (Fraser 1926). An early example of Arbitration that dealt with acts of expropriation was the Foreign Claims Settlement Commission created in the USA under the International Claims Act of 1949 (and its amendments of 1954 and 1958) (U.S. Department of Justice 2011). This Commission intended to provide compensation for the nationalisation or other taking of the property of American Nationals (Christie 1962). Arbitration Tribunals were set up to assess the claims of American nationals whose property was nationalised or suffered war damage in Bulgaria, Czechoslovakia, Hungary, Poland, Romania, Russia and Yugoslavia (Christie 1962). The functioning and the scope of the Tribunals were based upon agreements between the USA and the countries mentioned above.

Different arguments are presented about the benefits of investment arbitration. One such argument is that other instruments for the protection of foreign investors abroad such as diplomatic protection involve a high degree of politicisation. If diplomatic protection is exercised, it can jeopardise international relations among countries or the rights of the investor. Hence, it is argued, that investment arbitrations depoliticise investor's claims making it more useful for the protection of the rights of foreign investors while maintaining stable diplomatic relations among countries. Other arguments are that arbitrators are better qualified and have better skills and knowledge than domestic judges in peripheral countries to resolve a dispute. Finally, arbitration is presented as the best option as it allows the existence of a neutral and independent forum whenever a conflict arises between the foreign investor and the host state (Greider 2001).

Investment Arbitral Tribunals act as administrative courts judging the legality or illegality of an action adopted by any public authority of the host state. In other words, they legally assess acts *jure imperii*. The assessment pursued by Investment Arbitral Tribunals can be classified into two different types: sole effect and police power doctrines. In the case of the 'sole effect doctrine', arbitration tribunals focus on the effect of the sovereign act on the rights and interests of foreign investors, and compare it with the wording of the IIA (Isakoff 2013; Dolzer and Bloch, Indirect Expropriation: Conceptual Realignments?' 2003, (5) 155 2003).

In the case of the 'police powers doctrine', the Investment Tribunal not only considers the effects of the act upon the foreign investor. It also considers the context surrounding the act, including the purpose of the measure and giving weight to the sovereign right to regulate (Mostafa 2008).

Accordingly, investment arbitration has a direct impact on the domestic regulatory sphere. Through Investment Arbitration, which is essential for the success of the regime, countries are forced to comply with the commitments agreed upon in their IIAs. It is important to note how an arbitral procedure puts two very different parties with different interests, obligations and rights, domestically and internationally, in the same *locus standi*. The IIL system, allows companies holding millions of dollars to challenge measures adopted by a state that is acting on behalf of millions of people. The existing relationship between the host state and the foreign investor at the arbitral procedure is asymmetrical allowing the market and its main actors to confront governments and their laws (Foucault 2008).

There are many problematic aspects to the intrusion of investment arbitration tribunals within host states. One criticism against arbitral tribunals is that they do not have any multilateral state mandate, as is the case with other international tribunals such as the International Court of Justice (ICJ) the World Trade Organisation (WTO) Appellate Body or ad hoc international criminal tribunals such as the Rwanda Tribunal (ICTR). This affects the legitimacy of the tribunals. Moreover, the lack of permanence of the arbitrators facilitates the creation of economic incentives to act in a certain manner so as to secure a future appointment which, accordingly, translates into securing future income (Harten 2008). This has cast doubts upon the neutrality and objectivity of decisions adopted by arbitrators as the economic benefit of future appointments can influence a decision adopted by an arbitrator (Harten 2008). Another aspect worth noting is the revolving door and conflicts of interest as lawyers could act as both arbitrators and attorneys, and also as they could represent the interests of host states in one case and the interests of foreign investors in another (Langford, Behn and Lie 2017).

A further source of criticism relates to procedural issues. One continuous criticism has been the lack of an appeal instance that could create a form of consistent jurisprudence, facilitating the understanding of the scope of terms within treaties and also facilitating the actions of stakeholders, especially host states (Odumosu 2006–2007).[4] Another important criticism has focused on the lack of access to the procedure by third interested parties such as local communities affected by the decision of the arbitral tribunal (Prieto-Rios and Rivas 2020) (Levine 2011). The arguments lie in broadening the scope of

---

[4] The only option is to seek the revision by the ICSID tribunal (if the arbitral procedure was ICISID) or to seek the annulment of the award before a domestic court, which globally is a difficult procedure.

participation beyond the existing system of *amicus curiae* in instances such as ICSID guaranteeing proper participation in favour of the transparency of investment procedures.

Two other important criticisms against investment arbitration include the costs of the Arbitral Tribunal as well as the amount of money that the host state is obliged to pay as compensation, whenever it is found guilty of breaching treaty obligations. In both cases, it is argued that those factors can exercise considerable pressure on the host state at the moment it considers a present or future regulatory policy or decision. In terms of costs, it is calculated that the average cost for a host state to defend itself before an international investment arbitral tribunal could oscillate between US$1.5 and US$2.5 million (K. Tienhaara 2006). Compensation is also an important matter for the investor and the host state as, on the one hand, it can significantly affect the budget of the host country and, on the other, it represents for the investor the possibility of continuing to accumulate capital and reducing losses. Depending on the circumstances, compensation could reach some hundred million dollars (Miles 2015). For instance, in the case of *Mobil et al. v Venezuela* the Tribunal ordered the country to pay US$1.6 billion *(Venezuela Holdings, B.V., et al (case formerly known as Mobil Corporation, Venezuela Holdings, B.V., et al.) v. Bolivarian Republic of Venezuela 2014)*. In the infamous case of *Occidental v Ecuador*, the Tribunal initially ordered the country to pay to the foreign investor US$2.3 billion, sum that was later reduced to US$1.061billion *(Occidental Petroleum Corporation and Occidental Exploration and Production Company v. The Republic of Ecuador 2012)*. Furthermore, a host state can be sued by several investors based upon the same facts, which means the possibility of a host state having to pay compensation to several different investors. For instance, this was the lamentable situation that Argentina faced after the economic havoc experienced in 2001.

Although decisions reached by arbitration tribunals cannot overturn a national law, the amounts imposed as compensation may, however, generate a direct impact on domestic policy, giving priority to economic interests (Greider 2001). It is difficult to empirically conclude, without an extensive representative sample, whether investors could use arbitration as a method of putting pressure on host countries to behave or act in a certain way by forcing the host country to modify or to withdraw certain policy or norm. However, few examples such as the research carried out by Gus Van Harten in Canada or the case of Indonesia support the claim that the costs inherent to the arbitral procedure as well as the costs of compensation imposed upon the host country may persuade a host country to change or withdraw a policy or a norm creating a regulatory chill effect (Harten and Scott 2016).

In the case of Indonesia, the government enacted regulations imposing obligations on mining companies to protect the forest by forbidding open mining. In response to the new regulation, mining companies filed a complaint before the Indonesian government, arguing that the regulations were in breach of BITs. Because of this, the Indonesian government was forced to enact new legislation exempting from the mining prohibition previous mining companies that already possessed holder licenses (K. Tienhaara 2006).

What investment arbitration is doing is standardising a mechanism to resolve investment disputes world-wide based on Western cultural, political and economic principles, and overturning differences while offering a unique universal jurisdiction to foreign investors. To sum up, the system of arbitration thus delineated ends up functioning as a deterrent that prevents states from using its regulatory powers whenever such use might enter into conflict with the maximal interpretation of property that informs the system. Put otherwise, states are challenged to pay to regulate.

CONCLUSION

As discussed in this chapter, IIAs and Investment Arbitral Tribunals have allowed MNCs 'to impose on developing countries their view of a liberal and protective international framework, which the customary process failed to achieve' (Wouters, Sanderijn and Hachez 2013, 25). In this form, treaties and arbitral investment tribunals are limiting the sovereignty of peripheral host states specially affecting developing countries. However, these investment arbitral tribunals are not only temporary – not permanent – but also they do not have any multilateral state mandate as other international tribunals such as ICJ, the WTO Appellate Body or an ad hoc criminal tribunal such as the Rwanda Tribunal.

Furthermore, the system imposes an important burden as host states are expected to comply with the terms incorporated in IIAs. Host states are placed in a position of balancing international obligations towards the foreign investor, which in the majority of cases has little or no consideration for the social and economic conditions of the host state, nor of its duty towards its citizens and other commitments under international law such as the protection of the environment or the protection of Human Rights (Wouters, Sanderijn, and Hachez 2013, 47).

Finally, it is important to mention that the arguments and reasons used to legitimise the IIL system miss the point that the whole regime is part of a political and ideological international framework that, as a response to processes of decolonisation in the twentieth century, is in place to protect a capitalist system based upon inequality, plunder and unjustified global appropriation of surplus. It also serves to hide collective fantasies and notions of epistemic and racial superiority that inform the kinds of geo-political interventionist relations, social, legal and economic, impinging upon the ability of so-called 'Third World countries' to forge futures of their own as well as the moral image of a more integral humanity (Cornell 2008). In the end, the riddle of treaties and awards hides the fact that the whole IIL system facilitates situations of systemic violence in developing countries.

Chapter 4

The Encrypted Discourse of International Investment Law
Hierarchy, Knowledge and Power

International law today offers a wide variety of specialist vocabularies and institutions with which we engage in legal practice. Very often, as David Kennedy has observed, we commit to them without reflecting on their effects in the world of outcomes. (Martti Koskenniemi 2009)

INTRODUCTION

Following the analysis provided in the previous chapter on clauses common to International Investment Agreements (IIA) and the general function of Investor-State Dispute Settlement (IISD), this chapter explores the encryption of the International Investment Law (IIL) system. Specifically, in this chapter, I analyse the language embedded in IIA which is replicated by investment tribunals at the moment at which they assess the legality of an act implemented by a host state but which could affect the economic interests of foreign investors. In doing so, this chapter shows that the encryption of the system facilitates situations of systemic violence.

Of course, the use of the word 'encryption' may come as a surprise to the reader. The surprise is fully justified as the word 'encrypted'/'encryption' is commonly used within the context of governmental and military communications as well as in computing systems. In those contexts, encryption aims at protecting relevant information from unauthorised access by third parties (outsiders) through the encoding of information.

Encrypting a message allows two or more parties to communicate safely over a channel that might be 'tapped' by an outsider party (Goldreich 2004; Landau 2004). Encryption guarantees that outsiders (wire-tappers) are kept in ignorance about the communication between the interested parties. The protection of the information is materialised in the form of the parties knowing something that the outsiders (wire-tappers) cannot access and as such are unable to fully understand. The encryption of a message allows that only the interested parties can decrypt the encrypted message using certain codes acquired either as result of a specific training or by comprising part of a certain epistemological community (Goldreich 2004).

In the specific case of the IIL system, the term 'encryption' is used to explain the construction of an uncanny specific code-discourse based upon vagueness and technicality. The IIL system is an uncanny specific code-discourse that, to a regular non-initiated bystander, causes confusion as she sees how words that have seemed familiar and comfortable suddenly become unfamiliar and frightening before those non-initiated eyes (Suk 2008; Rahimi 2013). This frightening feeling is the result of an apprehension of something visually familiar, but at the same time incomprehensible, generating intellectual uncertainty (Freud 1919; Suk 2008). The uncanny of the IIL discourse serves to hide issues of epistemic superiority, a struggle for economic power in a globalised world and, as already mentioned, the concealment of the existence of economic violence.

In this form, non-initiated (outsiders) are prevented from having unauthorised access, understanding and use of the IIL discourse while at the same time hiding the violence attributable to the system by reason of it giving priority to economic interests. In addition, the use of the term 'encrypted/encryption', also allows the characterisation of an epistemic elite that is legitimated to decrypt the encrypted discourse holding the keys of interpretation of the IIL discourse.[1]

AN ENCRYPTED DISCOURSE

For the purpose of this chapter, 'discourse' is understood as a fictional construction that groups and organises words under a specific linguistic structure which can be articulated so as to communicate ideas and command actions, in

---

[1] It is important to mention that I wrote a previous reflection on this matter in the book *Decrypting Power* edited by Ricardo Sanin-Restrepo under the title *Encrypted International Investment Law* published by Rowman &Littlefield.

a verbal or written form, grounded upon a socio-historical basis.[2] Discourses are 'sanctioned-by a wide variety of highly visible organizational and socio-linguistic insignia of hierarchy, status power and wealth' (Goodrich 1987, 171), where only a few are entitled to create and interpret the discourse creating epistemic segregation.

Encryption of the IIL discourse does not mean secrecy or complete invisibility; rather it refers to something that is visible but vanishes, becoming unintelligible and uncanny (McCloskey 1995). In this regard, Derrida offers the following explanation:

> One can always reveal to the gaze something that still remains secret because its secret is accessible only to senses other than sight. For example, there might be some writing that I can't decipher (a letter in Chinese or Hebrew, or simply some undecipherable handwriting) but that remains perfectly visible in spite of its being sealed to most readers. It isn't hidden but it is encoded or encrypted. That which is hidden, as that which remains inaccessible to the eye or the hand, is not necessarily encrypted in the derivative senses of that word ciphered, coded, to be interpreted – in contrast to being hidden in the shadows (which is what it also meant in Greek) (Derrida 1995, 89).

In the specific case of IIL discourse, the words written in the treaties and awards are encrypted. The words on their own are intelligible and comprehensible (being familiar to the non-initiated); however, the words put together in the mentioned documents, become uncanny. The uncanniness of the IIL discourse highlights the fact that non-initiated is intellectually dependent upon the initiated (Rahimi 2013).

The encryption of the IIL discourse implies the production of unknowledge, or what Eduardo Mendieta refers to as 'epistemologies of ignorance' (Mendieta 2011; Prieto-Rios and Koram 2015). Epistemologies of ignorance (or agnotology) refer to intentional processes to create lacunas and to obscure knowledge (Mendieta 2015). In this regard, Eduardo Mendieta mentions the following: 'to know is to see while seeing what is not seen because it was looked at with a certain gaze' (Mendieta 2011, 253).

The encryption of the IIL discourse can be represented in the following diagram that shows the different level of encryption of the IIL discourse:

---

[2] This understanding of discourse draws from the reading of the works of Michele Foucault, *The Archaeology of Knowledge & the Discourse on Language* (A.M. Sheridan Smith, Pantheon Books, 1972); Peter Goodrich, *Legal Discourse: Studies in Linguistic, Rhetoric and Legal Analysis* (Palgrave Macmillan UK, 1987); and Michel Pecheux, *Language, Semantics and Ideology: Stating the Obvious* (Harbans Nagpal (tr), The MacMillan Press Ltd., 1982).

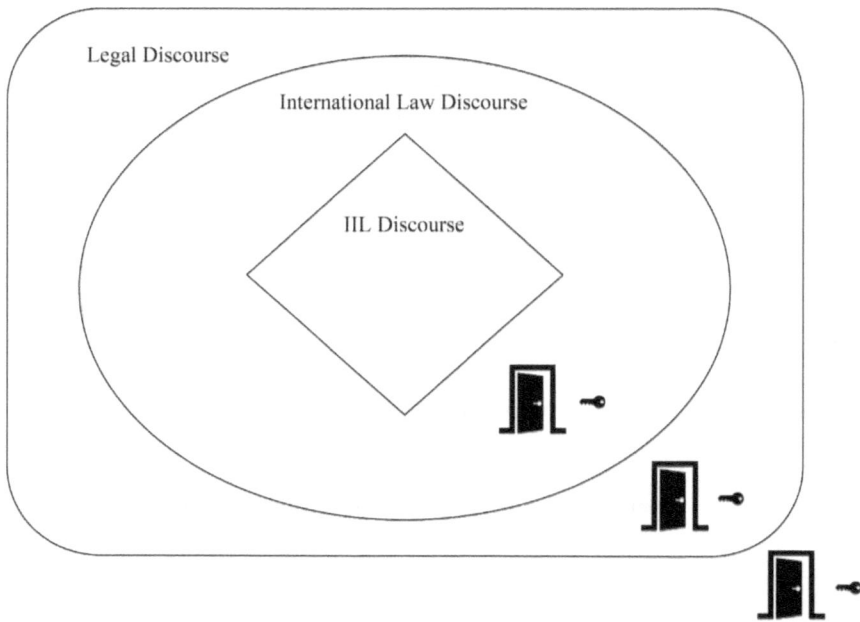

Knowing produces unknowing, in other words, the production of knowledge also implies the production of unknowledge or epistemologies of ignorance and the creation of blind spots. In the case of IIL, it is a production of knowledge surrounding the protection of the rights and interests of foreign investors. However, it also creates normative blindness that restricts participation in the production of its discourse. The normative blindness characterises the exclusion of social and cultural (pluralism) factors while maintaining relationships of unequal power that is represented by the difference between holders of knowledge, such as arbitrators, and non-holders of knowledge (Mattei and Nader 2008).

The encryption of the IIL discourse characterises the existing dialectical relationship between technicality and vagueness seen in IIA and arbitral awards. The encryption of the IIL discourse limits the possibility of broad public access and understanding, thus limiting public accountability. In this form, IIA and arbitral awards become 'nothing else than an encrypted document[s] for those that do not possess the knowledge' (Mendez Hincapíe and Sanín-Restrepo 2012).

The encryption of the discourse creates a widespread perception that the reality surrounding IIL is complex and traumatic, thus allowing the concealment of relationships of power (Mendez Hincapíe and Sanín-Restrepo 2012; Goodrich 1987). The IIL discourse transforms itself into something visible but not understood by the many, while only few are legitimately initiated to interpret it, they being the holders of the relevant juridical knowledge and as such, key holders of any interpretation (Goodrich 1987, 52). Arguments of technicality, objectivity and neutrality serve to distract the uninitiated, granting the authority and power of interpretation to those very few comprising the initiated, thereby creating barriers of exclusion (F. Fanon 2004; Mendez Hincapíe and Sanín-Restrepo 2012).

The encryption of the IIL discourse grants the power of deciphering and decrypting the discourse to the initiated that holds the key to the knowledge (explained in greater detail in the next section). The initiated are those tasked with decrypting the discourse that offers solutions to existing conflicts between foreign investors and host states. Furthermore, the initiated are perceived as the saviours who have a real dimension and understanding of the complex problems related to IIL (Mendez Hincapíe and Sanín-Restrepo 2012).

DIALECTICS OF VAGUENESS AND TECHNICALITY

As mentioned in the previous section, IIL discourse characterises a dialectical relationship of technicality and vagueness that renders it an encrypted discourse. Technicality (or technical language) in the sense that certain linguistic forms used in IIA, arbitral awards, reports or academic texts dedicated to this specific discipline (materialised in words as parts of sentences) are not in widespread use but, rather, are specific to this field of knowledge. This applies also, in the sense that the terminology is presented as the only feasible option of wording within IIL (McSwain, Orion F. White and Bruce 1989).

'Vagueness' applies in the sense that its content and meaning are broad and is, consequently, open to any interpretation. In this respect, Anthea Roberts mentions the following:

> Investment treaties have traditionally been short and vaguely worded, while the system as a whole is new and under theorized (Roberts 2013) . . . As investment treaties create broad standards rather than specific rules, they must be interpreted before they can be applied. Investor-state tribunals have accordingly played a critical role in interpreting, hence developing, investment treaty law (Roberts 2013).

Some parts of the terminology of the IIL discourse demonstrate the duality described above (i.e. technicality and vagueness) including, among others investor, investment, public order, essential security interests, fair and equitable treatment (FET), legitimate expectations, umbrella clauses, most-favoured nation (MFN) and indirect expropriation. It is important to indicate as a fact, that these terms and clauses have become virtually universal in the entire global network of IIAs (Miles 2015).

These terms, which are simply sequences of words, are claims for legal certainty and the protection of foreign investments against measures adopted by the host state that could affect investor's interests as protected by IIA. In this form, the full set of words represent a form of risk management offering protection against unpredictable political or legal risks thereby securing investor's profits.

The words and sentences incorporated in IIA are interpreted by arbitrators sitting in an Investment Arbitral Tribunal. As will be explained in greater detail in section 4 of this chapter, arbitrators make up part of the group of initiated, who are entitled to decipher the encrypted discourse.

In the case of investment arbitral awards, they are adopted by arbitral tribunals, which depending upon the terms of the treaty, could be either an *ad hoc* tribunal or an institutional tribunal. The *ad hoc* tribunal acts independently of any international institution and depends entirely upon the regulations agreed upon by the parties. On the other hand, the institutional tribunal is linked to organisations which specialise in matters of arbitral procedures; the most commonly employed for that purpose are the International Centre for Settlement of Investment Disputes (ICSID) and the Paris based International Chamber of Commerce (ICC).

In investment arbitration, the principle (or rule) of precedent does not exist, as the award has an *inter partes* effect and investment tribunals are not bound by previous decisions reached by other investment arbitral tribunals.[3] However, the lack of precedent does not mean that arbitrators in their decisions do not consider previous awards or even a consistent jurisprudence. However, the non-existence of a precedent allows for the existence of different interpretations and makes the discourse more encrypted as it is extremely difficult to foresee the way in which certain treaty clauses are going to be interpreted by arbitrators.[4]

In the following lines, out of the 1023 known investment treaty arbitration cases, (up to 2019) (United Nations Conference on Trade and Development

---

[3] For instance, article 1136 (1) of NAFTA expressly establishes that an 'award made by a Tribunal shall have no binding force except between the disputing parties and in respect of the particular case'.

[4] Some academics such as Susan Franck argue that the reason for the lack of uniformity in decisions reached by investment arbitral tribunals is the fact that the system is still in its infancy; Susan D. Franck, 'The Legitimacy Crisis in Investment Treaty Arbitration: Privatizing Public International Law Through Inconsistent Decisions', (2005) 73 (4), *Fordham Law Review* 1521 considers this to be a mild argument to describe the reality in which there is an encryption of the system for which the non-existence of precedent highly contributes. In this form, the vagueness and technicality of the IIL discourse permits the encryption of the regime and allows words could be interpreted in different forms.

2020, 110), I will present some cases by way of examples to see the complexities related to the encryption of the IIL's discourse. The analysis will commence with the three cases known as the 'Argentinean Saga' that deal with 'fair and equitable treatment' and regulatory expropriation (Schneiderman 2013). These investment cases derived from the decision taken by the Argentine Government to freeze the convertibility of tariffs into U.S. dollars in order to tackle the 2000 economic crisis.

The first case of the 'Argentinean Saga' relates to *Argentina v. CMS Gas* (CMS). In this case a Michigan-based company purchased 30 per cent of the public company Transportada de Gas del Norte (TGN). The purchase was the result of processes of privatisation pursued by the Argentine government (Schneiderman 2010). The argument advanced by CMS was that the convertibility of profits into pesos instead of dollars considerably reduced their profits. Furthermore, the Argentine government had guaranteed an investment return regardless of the economic situation experienced by the country, but was failing to do so, thus creating a situation of indirect expropriation and violation of the standard of fair and equitable treatment (FET). The government of Argentina argued that it had acted under a state of necessity which was an exception recognised by Customary International Law as well as by article XI of the USA-Argentina Bilateral Investment Treaty (BIT).

The arbitral tribunal held that although there was no indirect expropriation, there was a clear denial of the principle of FET that entitled CMS to receive compensation (*CMS Gas Transmission Company v. The Republic of Argentina* 2005). The tribunal also held that necessity could not be a defence if there were other available options for the host country even if those option were costlier. According to the tribunal, article XI was in place to allow the host state to take measures only 'in the event of total economic and social collapse' rather than merely a 'severe crisis' (*CMS Gas Transmission Company v. The Republic of Argentina* 2005; Schneiderman, *Judicial Politics and International Investment Arbitration: Seeking an Explanation for Conflicting Outcomes* 2010). The tribunal awarded CMS US$132.2 million with interest and US$2.1 million upon transfer of its shares in TGN to Argentina (*CMS Gas Transmission Company v. The Republic of Argentina* 2005).

The second case of the Argentine saga is the case of *LG & E Capital Corp. and LG & E International, Inc. v. Argentine Republic* (*LG & Energy Corp., LG&E Capital Corp. and LG&E International, Inc. v. Argentine Republic* 2008). LG & E was a company based in Kentucky, USA, seeking damages because of the above measures adopted in 2000 by the Argentine government to protect its economy. The investment arbitration, as in the CMS case (above) upheld the duty of the host country to maintain the stability of the legal and business framework as 'an essential element in the standard of what is fair and equitable treatment' (*LG & Energy Corp., LG&E Capital Corp.*

and *LG&E International, Inc. v. Argentine Republic* 2008). Nonetheless, in this award, the tribunal accepted that article XI of the USA-Argentina BIT, which refers to the state of necessity, would allow a host state such Argentina to adopt certain measures to protect the social and economic system. Specifically, the Tribunal stated the following:

> [A]n economic recovery package was the only means to respond to the crisis. Although there may have been a number of ways to draft the economic recovery plan, the evidence before the Tribunal demonstrates that an across the board response was necessary, and the tariffs on public utilities had to be addressed (*LG & Energy Corp., LG&E Capital Corp. and LG&E International, Inc. v. Argentine Republic* 2008).

Argentina was found to be partially liable and was required to pay as reparation the sum of US $57.4 million (including interest) to the foreign investor. The amount did not include the period between December 2001 and April 2003 which corresponded to the beginning of the crisis until the election of Nestor Kirchner, President of Argentine for the period 2003–2007.

Finally, in this saga of Argentine cases, is the dispute of *Enron Corporation and Ponderosa Assets, LP v. Argentine Republic (Enron Corporation and Ponderosa Assets, LP. v. Argentine Republic 2007)*. In this case, the tribunal rejected the argument of necessity put forward by the Argentine government because the interpretation of the state of necessity was different to the decision of LG & E Capital Corp. The arbitral tribunal concluded that there was a clear denial of the FET treatment by the host government, and awarded damages equivalent to U.S. $106.2 million. The tribunal considered that other possible measures to respond to the economic crisis were available to the state and argued that the government of Argentina had contributed to the economic situation experienced by the country (*Enron Corporation and Ponderosa Assets, LP. v. Argentine Republic* 2007).

Moving beyond the Argentine Saga, there is the case of *Tokios Tokelés v Ukraine.* Tokios Tokelés was a company 99 per cent controlled and owned by Ukrainian nationals and incorporated in Lithuania. This was the first occasion in investment arbitration in which a tribunal had to address a dispute raised by a company controlled by citizens of the responding state. At first glance, one could assume that since investment arbitration tribunals are meant to resolve international disputes between a State and a foreign investor, the company should be barred from accessing arbitration. However, contrary to that plausible assumption, the decision by the arbitral tribunal studying the dispute deemed that, for the effects of the Lithuania-Ukraine BIT, the company had to be considered as Lithuanian and the origin of the capital was irrelevant.

The main argument used by the arbitral tribunal was that the test of incorporation[5] was agreed by the parties in the Lithuania-Ukraine BIT as to the correct mechanism to establish the nationality of a legal person. It is worth noting that this decision was criticised by the chairman of the tribunal who, in his dissenting opinion, considered that this was contrary to the object and purpose of the ICSID Convention, seeing that the origin of the capital was relevant and decisive in the assessment of the international character of an investor (*Tokios Tokelés v. Ukraine*, Dis. Op. 2004).

The issue of claims by dual nationals has also seen inconsistent decisions in arbitration tribunals constituted under UNCITRAL Arbitration Rules regarding physical persons. On the one hand, in the case *Serafín García v. Venezuela*, the tribunal upheld its jurisdiction regarding a claim by investors that held both Spanish and Venezuelan nationalities. The tribunal declined to subject the nationality of the investors to the effective or predominant nationality test applicable under public international law which, in this case, was the Venezuelan nationality given that Venezuela was the residence country of both of the investors and the birthplace of one of them (*Serafín García Armas and Karina García Gruber v. Bolivarian Republic of Venezuela* 2014). On the other hand, in the case *Rawat v. Mauritius*, the tribunal considered that the Mauritian nationality of the investor was predominant over the French one and that, in interpreting the BIT in accordance with the context, it should consider the ICSID Convention exclusion of dual nationals from the concept of foreign investors. As such, the tribunal declined its jurisdiction (*Dawood Rawat v. The Republic of Mauritius 2018*).

Another relevant example for our study of the technicality and vagueness of discourse is the interpretation of what is to be considered an investment (Yannaca-Small and Liberti 2008). The meaning of the term 'investment' varies according to each investment treaty (Yannaca-Small and Liberti 2008). In the case *Link-Trading v. Department for Customs of Republic of Moldova* based on the 1993 U.S.-Republic of Moldova BIT (and which was an ad hoc UNCITRAL arbitration), the claimant argued to have been the victim of a regulatory expropriation as a result of modifications to the Value Added Tax (VAT) exemptions and duties which affected the economic viability of the enterprise (*Link-Trading Joint Stock Company v. Department for Customs Control of the Republic of Moldova* 2002). The arbitral tribunal studied whether debt financing could be a form of investment. The Tribunal drew attention to article (1a) of the BIT that very broadly defined investment. The article appeared as follows:

---

[5] A company is considered to be a national of the country where it is incorporated.

> Every kind of investment in the territory of one Party owned or controlled directly or indirectly by [...] companies of the other Party, such as equity, debt, and service and investment contracts; and includes: (i) tangible and intangible property [...] (V) any right conferred by law or contract, and any licences and permits pursuant to law. (*Link-Trading Joint Stock Company v. Department for Customs Control of the Republic of Moldova* 2002)

According to the Tribunal, the definition of investment was very broad and, as such, debt financing could be deemed to be a form of investment. Thus, the Tribunal recognised its jurisdiction over the dispute (*Link-Trading Joint Stock Company v. Department for Customs Control of the Republic of Moldova* 2002).

Another case related to the extent of the scope of investment, is the dispute of *SGS v. Pakistan*, that arose as a result of the non-payment of invoices to the Swiss company SGS for the services of pre-shipment inspection and certification services (*SGS Société Générale de Surveillance S.A. v. Islamic Republic of Pakistan* 2003). The arbitral tribunal, analysed, inter alia, whether the services provided by the company could be considered to be an investment.

According to the tribunal, considering the broad definition of investment established in the Switzerland-Pakistan BIT, which included claims for money derived from the law or from contracts, pre-shipment and inspection services fell under the broad definition of 'investment' established in the BIT (*SGS Société Générale de Surveillance S.A. v. Islamic Republic of Pakistan* 2003). Furthermore, the Tribunal also argued that considering the activity performed by the Swiss company, it was, as a concession, related to the management and collection of revenue in ports.

Moreover, in those cases in which the states have attempted to address the vagueness and technicality of the IIL discourse, arbitration tribunals have still managed to keep it intact. This occurred notably regarding the interpretation of the FET under the NAFTA. The NAFTA Free Trade Commission issued on 2001 an interpretative note according to which the obligation to comply with the FET obligation did not require an additional treatment or a treatment beyond that required under the customary international minimum standard. However, the NAFTA arbitration tribunals considered that the customary international minimum standard had evolved in such a way that the threshold for finding a violation was no longer high (*Mondev International Ltd. v. United States of America* 2002).

The content of the FET standard has given rise to a set of inconsistent decisions in arbitrations against Spain under the Energy Charter Treaty following measures adopted after 2010 that retracted some features of regulations intended to incentivise investment in renewable energy implemented in 2007. On the issue of legitimate expectations, the tribunal in *Charanne* decided that the framework established by Spain prior to 2010 was not enough to create legitimate expectations, while the tribunal in *Novenergia* considered the opposite, that is, that the original framework has created legitimate expectations (*Charanne and Construction Investments v. Spain* 2016; *Novenergia II v. The Kingdom of Spain* 2018). On the issue of the reasonable nature of the measures, the tribunal in *Isolux* decided that the conduct of the state was a rational policy aimed at the protection of the consumer, while the tribunal in Eiser held that the new measures were unreasonable (*Isolux Netherlands, BV v. Kingdom of Spain* 2016; *Eiser Infrastructure Limited and Energía Solar Luxembourg S.à r.l. v. Kingdom of Spain* 2017).

The foregoing examples not only show the encryption of the IIL discourse but also how encryption grants huge power to the arbitrators (the initiated) as they are the only and few holders of the juridical knowledge to interpret the treaty's obligations. In this form, IIL discourse transforms itself into a form of encrypted discourse that generates situations of obscurity, unintelligibility and exclusion where only few are entitled to understand the discourse.

THE INITIATED

Encrypted discourses are decrypted only by few initiated individuals who possess the keys to the knowledge (Mendieta 2011). The existence of the initiated is based upon an appropriation and enclosure of knowledge that creates a Manichean division between 'legitimate interpreters' with the right to interpret and speak (insiders) and 'illegitimate interpreters' (outsiders). In this form, the insiders transform themselves into a class of specialists, or initiated, deemed as experts, legitimated to speak, to encrypt and to decrypt the IIL discourse. In this context, Michelle Foucault states the following:

> Who is speaking? Who, among the totality of speaking individuals, is accorded the right to use this sort of language? Who is qualified to do so? Who derives from it his own special quality, his prestige, and from whom, in return, does he receive if not the assurance, at least the presumption that what he says is true? What is the status of the individuals who – alone – have the right, sanctioned by law or tradition, juridically defined or spontaneously accepted, to proffer such a discourse? (M. Foucault 1972, 50)

> This authority also involves the rules and processes of appropriation of discourse: for in our societies (and no doubt in many others) the property of discourse – in the sense of the right to speak, ability to understand, licit, and immediate access to the corpus of already formulated statements, and the capacity to invest this discourse in decisions, institutions, or practices – is in fact

confined (sometimes with the addition of legal sanctions) to a particular group of individuals (M. Foucault 1972, 68).

In the case of IIL discourse, the initiated, those legitimated to decrypt the encrypted discourse can be classified into two distinct categories: that is 'observer interpreters' and 'decision-making interpreters'. 'Observer interpreters' are those initiated who understand the encrypted discourse, can offer opinions but who have limited influence in the functioning of the regime and as such do not hold all the keys to decrypting the encrypted discourse.

The category of observer interpreters includes academics, politicians and activists who are directly or indirectly involved in the creation of investment treaties and in the analysis of the effects and the rationale of arbitral awards. Individuals in this category allow communications between the system and the rest of the community (outsiders). On the other hand, there are 'decision-making interpreters' who correspond to that small group of individuals who are 'the legitimate interpreters' and are, as such, the ones who hold the keys to decrypt the encrypted IIL discourse. Under this label comes the legal advisers who draft the terms of treaties (BITs/FTAs) and the arbitrators.

Considering time and space limits, I will focus on 'decision-making interpreters,' specifically investment arbitrators. They are essential to understanding the dynamics of IIL's discourse as well as the different directions taken by the system. Investment arbitrators exercise significant material influence in the IIL system (Langford, Behn and Lie 2017).

Investment arbitrators constitute an international elite group that is attached to an exclusive market of high-stakes disputes in which the fate of investors and countries are in the hands of those very few initiated (Kapeliuk 2010). Investment arbitrators are self-regulated professionals that 'serve as decision-makers for cases under multiple institutions and act as counsel in other proceedings across the globe' (Puig 2014).

Access to become a member of the selected group of the initiated is restricted to a small world-wide elite which uses 'strictly rhetorical settings of legal communications and contacts with the non-legal world' (Goodrich 1987, 152). Moreover, distinct levels of involvement also exist between investment arbitrators, a difference between those who are appointed once, or a very few times, and those who are constantly appointed to arbitration panels (Kapeliuk 2010). The existence of a strong core group of arbitrators who are appointed several times in arbitral panels reflects their power and their influence in the system (Langford, Behn and Lie 2017).

Different empirical works have analysed the dynamics within the world of investment arbitrators. These empirical works offer a glimpse into the functioning of the restricted club of the initiated within IIL system. In the following lines, some of those works will be presented.

The first empirical study to be referred to is the work of Susan Franck. In her research, Franck used 102 arbitration awards as a sample (up to June 2006) and her findings concluded that, out of 145 arbitrators, 82 Arbitrators were from North American or Western European countries. The division of the data shows the following: twenty-seven arbitrators were from the USA, fourteen from the United Kingdom, eight from Canada, eight from France, six from Germany, six from Sweden, five from Italy, five from Switzerland and four from Spain (Franck, Empirically Evaluating Claims About Investment Treaty Arbitration 2007).

Daphna Kapeliuk in her research found that in 105 out of 131 concluded ICSID cases, 26 arbitrators had been appointed four or more times either as a party arbitrator or president compared with 107 arbitrators who were appointed only once (the total number of arbitrators in her study was 175) (Kapeliuk 2010). Kapeliuk's research also found that the majority of elite ICSID arbitrators came from North American or Western European countries. Under this analysis, the figures show that out of twenty-six elite arbitrators appointed four or more times in ICSID arbitral panels, seventeen were from North America or Western Europe. Those arbitrators came from the following countries: five from France, three from Canada, two from Switzerland, two from the USA, one from Spain, one from the UK, one from the Netherlands, one from Italy and one from Germany (Kapeliuk 2010).

On the issue of gender, Kapeliuk found that among the twenty-six elite arbitrators (those who were appointed at least four times for ICSID procedures) only two were women (Kapeliuk 2010). Similarly, Franck's research found that out of 145 investment treaty arbitrators only 3.5 per cent (five) were women (Gabrielle Kaufman-Kohler, Sandra Rico, Carolyn Lamm, Guidetta Moss and Tatiana de Maekelt). They were appointed only for an equivalent of 11 per cent (9) of the awards analysed by Franck (Franck, Empirically Evaluating Claims About Investment Treaty Arbitration 2007–2008).

The third research is the one carried out by Sergio Puig, who analysed all the appointments made in proceedings under ICSID between 1972 and February 2014, he carried out interviews with arbitration professionals and created a database (Puig 2014). In his study, he identified that 419 different arbitrators from eight-seven countries sat on ICSID tribunals and ad hoc Committees. Out of the 419, 93 per cent were male and from seven Western countries (New Zealand, Australia, Canada, Switzerland, France, the United Kingdom and the USA) representing almost half of total appointments (Puig 2014).

The fourth relevant research was conducted by Malcolm Langford, Daniel Behn and Runar Hilleren Lie. In their research, they highlight how 'international investment arbitration is marked by a revolving door: individuals act sequentially and even simultaneously as arbitrator, legal counsel, expert witness, or tribunal secretary' (Langford, Behn and Lie 2017).

For this research, the authors analysed 1,039 international investment arbitration cases and ICSID4 annulment proceedings using the PluriCourts Investment Treaty Arbitration Database (PITAD) as at 1 January 2017. They identified, that out of the top twenty-five arbitrators (only two women among them) twenty-one came from Western States (Langford, Behn and Lie 2017).

The data presented above confirms that IIL is an encrypted regime, based on Western legal principles and rules and which continues to be in the hands of Western experts and as such under Western epistemology. It also shows that the investment arbitrator community is a closed one and interaction is kept among that epistemic/professional community (Langford, Behn and Lie 2017).

It is important to note that there are also investment arbitrators from developing countries serving as members of arbitral panels. However, as the IIL regime is founded upon Western legal conceptions and institutions, the process of decrypting the IIL discourse is framed within those epistemological boundaries, not giving much room for interpretation outside the Western legal epistemology. Arbitrators from developing countries use and re-enact a language of oppression created by the legal and intellectual elite of the metropolis (F. Fanon 2004). Arbitrators as part of an elite of developing countries are moulded by the Western legal culture living materially and intellectually in the Western legal culture (Cabral 2016). It is important to highlight that most of the individuals from developing countries that participate in this close community have had their studies in Western countries (Puig 2014).

Learning and mastering the discourse does not necessarily mean influencing or making profound changes to the entire system, there is only a process of appropriation of the IIL discourse. Arbitrators from developing countries do nothing different than perform a process of creolisation of knowledge (Gordon 2015). Training and indoctrination play an important role in the Westernisation of Third World arbitrators that participate in the IIL arbitral structure. Fanon describes very well the effects of the process of indoctrination of intellectuals in peripheral countries:

> The native intellectual accepted the cogency of these ideas, and deep down in his brain you could always find a vigilant sentinel ready to defend the Greco-Latin pedestal. (F. Fanon 2004)

The universalisation of the legal tradition necessarily means that legal operators are raised and train within those parameters, and become instruments of and for the continuation of the western normative monopoly (F. Fanon 2004). Furthermore, it is important to consider that in the process of decrypting the encrypted discourse, ideology plays a very important role, as Michel Pecheux states:

> [T]here are contrasting 'vocabularies-syntaxes' and 'arguments', which lead, sometimes with the same words, in different directions depending on the nature of the ideological interest at stake. (Pecheux 1982, 111) ... words, expressions, propositions, etc., change their meaning according to the positions held by those who use them, which signifies that they find their meaning by reference to those positions, i.e., by reference to ideological formations. (Pecheux 1982, 111)

The articulation happens in the form of ideology interpellating the individual and the subject, giving meaning to the encrypted linguistic formations. Pecheux, adds the following:

> [I]ndividuals are interpellated as speaking subject (as subjects of their discourse) by the discursive formations which represent 'in language' the ideological formations that correspond to them, and I specified that the interpellation of the individual as subject of his discourse is achieved by the identification (of the subject) with the discursive formation that dominates him. (Pecheux 1982, 156)

The ideology that directs how the IIL discourse is decrypted and interpreted is neoliberalism. The initiated may not recognise the unconscious role played by neoliberalism as the hegemonic ideology which in its own has been bound by socio-historical dimensions (Goodrich 1987, 136). Rather, the initiated at the moment of decrypting the IIL discourse use arguments of neutrality and objectivity which are intertwined with technical-economist arguments as the fundaments of their decryption task.[6]

CONSEQUENCES

Different consequences come from the encryption of the IIL system. However, for reasons of space limit, I will focus my attention to those consequences that I consider are more relevant for this book´s argument. One of the first, consequences of the encryption is the confused application of the *Vienna Convention on the Law of Treaties* (*VCLT*). Article 31 paragraph 1 of VCLT states the following:

---

[6] I have borrowed the expression technicist-economist from Louis Althusser see Louis Althusser, *On the Reproduction of Capitalism: Ideology and Ideological State Apparatuses* (G.M. Goshgarian (tr) Verso, 2014), 44 and other pages.

> A treaty shall be interpreted in good faith in accordance with the ordinary meaning to be given to the terms of the treaty in their context and in the light of its object and purpose. (Vienna Convention on the Law of Treaties 1969)

At the moment that an Arbitral Tribunal interprets an IIA, which as mentioned, contains encrypted clauses, the rule of the 'ordinary meaning to the terms' cannot easily be applied as the combination of technicality and vagueness make it difficult or almost impossible to decide what the ordinary meaning of the words is in an IIA.

Another relevant consequence derived out of the system's encryption is that it creates a direct clash between the IIL system and other branches of Public International Law (PIL). Although it is clear that PIL is a fragmented system that requires rules for the interaction between its different branches, the encryption of the IIL, makes it difficult to put into practice the rules and instruments proposed by the International Law Commission (ILC) to resolve conflicts between the international obligations derived from IIA and the international obligations derived from other instruments such as Human Rights or Environmental treaties (Koskenniemi, Fragmentation of International Law: Difficulties Arising from the Diversification and Expansion of International Law 2006).

The third relevant consequence, directly linked to the previous one, is that it grants a priority to the government of the host country to freely decide how to handle the relationship between IIA and domestic norms and policies justifying itself within the IIA. In other words, IIA serves to justify domestic normative changes making it more economic-centric and more favourable to the investor´s interests (Perry-Kessaris 2008).

The fourth important consequence of the system's encryption is the encouragement of the phenomenon known as regulatory chill. This phenomenon consists of the willing decision of the state to neither act nor regulate certain events or matters that could interfere with the economic interest or rights of foreign investors, as protected by IIA, in order to avoid an international legal case before an international investment tribunal (Harten and Scott, Investment Treaties and the Internal Vetting of Regulatory Proposals: A Case Study from Canada 2016). This intentional inaction prioritises economic interest and the market over the protection of higher interests such as the protection of the environment or protection of human rights (Prieto-Rios, Gómez-Rey and Diaz-Chalela, Between the Environment and Foreign Investment Protection: the case of Santurban in ICSID 2019).

The lack of clarity and certainty of treaty interpretation as well as the huge sums imposed by the awards as compensations affects the sovereign powers of the host states. It also poses a threat to the whole system as it places in jeopardy the legitimacy of the system. Furthermore, it also facilitates situations of systemic violence in which politics and public interest are fully reduced to the negotiation of private interests, corrupting the basics of the traditional understanding of how democracy ought to operate (Zizek, Living in the End Times 2011, 55). It also creates a situation in which people around the world are directly or indirectly regulated and affected by the IIL system of which the majority is ignorant, and as such they need to trust in the interpretation given by the initiated who are the legitimated to decrypt the encrypted discourse.

CONCLUSION

This chapter has shown that the encryption of the IIL discourse becomes an intelligible but authoritative body of knowledge that facilitates forms of monopoly of knowledge contributing to maintaining unbalanced relationships of power (Rouse 2007). This situation allows relationships of power to be hidden, thus frustrating popular formations, creating areas of political and social exclusion and facilitating situations of social and political control (Mendez Hincapíe and Sanín-Restrepo 2012).

The relevance of unearthing the encryption of the IIL discourse, relates to the fact that in general the IIL system is a very particular one. First of all, there is no unified body such as the WTO where countries can discuss policies, there is no global treaty such as the Universal Declaration of Human Rights, but rather there is a network of at least 3,200 international treaties. Second, there is no single permanent court dealing with these matters such as the International Court of Justice or the WTO Appellate Body; issues are resolved by non-permanent arbitral tribunals.

Within this structure, only few, a very limited class of 'legally competent subjects', have the authority and power to create and to decrypt the encrypted discourse offering the right interpretation (Goodrich 1987, 81). As shown in this text, the interpreters (the initiated) are a global elite of arbitrators that come mainly from Western Europe or North America and so reinforce a single westernised functioning of the system. This form of the understanding of the regime has been dependent upon the initiated who maintain the status of dominance over the IIL discourse, which is also bound by neoliberal hegemonic ideology.

Moreover, as the encryption creates insiders and outsiders (legitimated and non-legitimated to speak the IIL's discourse), it limits political participation and the accountability of host states and their authorities. Nonetheless, capital-importer countries that on a global scale are politically and economically weaker, behave as 'good zombies' (Tostanova and

Mignolo 2009), continue negotiating IIAs. The challenge is then to move the IIL regime from using an encrypted discourse to a non-encrypted discourse, allowing wide participation and granting normative acknowledgement. Perhaps the first step towards this goal would be to look South to make the system more inclusive.

Chapter 5

Neoliberal Ideology
A Tale of Persistence and Hegemony

So in Chile the 'paternity' of the model has never been in dispute because as both supporters and adversaries agree that neo-liberalism has mainly been 'made in Chile'. (Silva 2006, 44)

INTRODUCTION

In the previous chapter, I analysed the encryption of the International Investment Law (IIL) discourse which facilitates situations of systemic violence. I also noted the very important role played by neoliberal ideology in the decryption process of the IIL encrypted discourse. Continuing along the same argumentative line, this chapter reflects on neoliberalism as a form of ideology that has a direct impact in the IIL system. This theoretical analysis contributes to broadening the scope of analysis as to how the IIL system facilitates systemic violence.[1]

The use of the term 'neoliberalism' in the social sciences has increased significantly over the last decade (Peck 2012, 13). Its use, however, remains inconsistent and sometimes confusing. It has been used as a synonym for the so-called 'Washington Consensus'; it is sometimes associated with establishment and mainstream politicians, or with the economic policies of the USA. Neoliberalism is also connected to an ideology, to refer to a form of discourse, or as a heterogeneous set of institutions. Perhaps, the different functions and meanings of 'neoliberalism' represent its complicated history

---

[1] I published an early version of this chapter in the Birkbeck Law Review titled: 'Neoliberal Market Rationality: The Driver of International Investment Law' (Prieto-Rios, Neoliberal Market Rationality: The Driver of International Investment Law, 2015).

as well as its malleability in occupying different spaces and in adapting to different realities (Peck 2012, 15).

For the purposes of this chapter, I analyse neoliberalism from the perspective of an ideological project that affects the intellectual subconscious of individuals who interact with the IIL system (Gary Gutting 2007). Accordingly, the argument presented here is that neoliberalism is not a mere economic project, but rather a hegemonic ideological project that affects the IIL system. It is reflected in the way in which International Investment Agreements (IIAs) are drafted as well as how the Investor-State Dispute Settlement system (ISDS) works.

Much of the literature has recognised the 1970s and 1980s as the golden age of neoliberalism (Fine 2009). It is important, however, to delve further back into the construction and development of neoliberalism as an ideology. Hence, we can analyse how this ideology evolved from being a marginal intellectual project, to becoming a hegemonic world-wide ideology, which has framed global political, legal and economic decisions including the functioning of the IIL system (Peck and Tickell, Neoliberalizing Space 2002).

The term 'neoliberalism' refers to an updated form of the economic liberalism of the eighteenth and nineteenth centuries that rejected the idea of any state intervention, other than to maintaining the peace and security of the country. Neoliberalism, conversely, accepts that governments play an important role in securing the rule of law that is an essential precondition for the correct functioning of the market (Birch and Mykhnenko 2010).

Neoliberalism as an ideology is characterised by its contradictory nature combining 'dogmatism and adaptability, strategic intent and opportunistic exploitation' (Peck, Constructions of Neoliberal Reason 2012, 4). It is also characterised by its promotion of the free market, entrepreneurism, extreme protection of property rights, reduction in social investment and limitation of the role of the state in the economy (De Sousa Santos 2002, 314). Neoliberal ideology also facilitates the naturalisation of certain relationships of power within the IIL and hides the violent colonial economic past of the IIL system and its existence as an instrument that facilitates forms of systemic violence (Coronil 2000).

ABOUT IDEOLOGY

Throughout history the term 'ideology' has been approached in different ways. In 1776, Destutt de Tracy introduced the term (ideology) during his lectures at the Institute to refer to the 'science of ideas' (Althusser, On the Reproduction of Capitalism: Ideology and Ideological State Apparatuses 2014, 171). The term used by Destutt referred to the development of a theory (logy) on the genesis of the ideas (ideo). The notion of the genesis of ideas played a significant role in the tradition of the philosophy of enlightenment (Althusser, On the Reproduction of Capitalism: Ideology and Ideological State Apparatuses 2014). In this regard Emmet Kennedy comments that

> Clear here is something which approaches the secular milleniarism of modern ideologies. 'Ideology' was, in the mind of its founders, more than the Greek translation of 'science des ideas'. It was a political and social ideology as well. (Kennedy 1979)

The meaning originally given by Tracy changed throughout the years (Gunder 2010); for instance, Frederic Engels approached ideology as a form of false consciousness, Lenin as class consciousness and Karl Mannheim as a form of a world-view. The different approaches to ideology led the term to reach its current understanding according to which 'ideology' is meant as a system of dominating ideas and representations (Althusser, On the Reproduction of Capitalism: Ideology and Ideological State Apparatuses 2014, 158). To develop the argument presented here, this chapter draws special attention to Althusser's conceptualisation of ideology. According to Althusser, ideology is perceived as a form of social cohesion that dominates the minds of interpellated subjects and which is materialised in their social interactions:

> Ideology is such an organic part of every social totality. Ideology is above all structures that they impose on the vast majority of men...Ideology is not a conceptual representation of the world, but the way we live that world at the level of unconscious. (Althusser, On the Reproduction of Capitalism: Ideology and Ideological State Apparatuses 2014, 253)

Accordingly, ideology has a material 'experience' that affects the material world where interpellated subjects interact; in other words, ideas that constitute a specific ideology do not have a spiritual existence, rather they have a material one (Althusser, On the Reproduction of Capitalism: Ideology and Ideological State Apparatuses 2014, 258). The material existence of ideology is different to the material existence of a weapon or a stone. As Althusser explains, matter 'exists in different modalities, all rooted in the last instance in "physical" matter' (Althusser, On the Reproduction of Capitalism: Ideology and Ideological State Apparatuses 2014, 259). In the case of ideology, it materialises in all the different actions and rituals performed by interpellated subjects (Althusser, On the Reproduction of Capitalism: Ideology and Ideological State Apparatuses 2014, 260). The ideology embodied in the apparatuses interpellates individuals who decide, in turn, to live in accordance with it (Zizek, Living in the End Times 2011, 13).

It is important to clarify that the term 'interpellation' (or hailing) refers to the process by which individuals are recruited by a specific ideology and are transformed into subjects (Althusser, On the Reproduction of Capitalism: Ideology and Ideological State Apparatuses 2014, 264). Althusser explains such an operation with the example of a 'police officer (or other) hailing an individual on the street: The police officer calls out the individual: "Hey you", and then the individual turns around 180 degrees responding to the officer's call' (Althusser, On the Reproduction of Capitalism: Ideology and Ideological State Apparatuses 2014). At that moment (the moment of turning), the individual becomes a subject; the individual is hailed by ideology.

Individuals hailed by a specific ideology accept, without reservations, the core principles of that specific form of ideology, as the only truth (Pecheux 1982). In this form, the hailed individual acts according to the principles of that particular ideology which then become something obvious or natural to the subject, and which determine the individual's interactions with the world. This normalisation of the hegemonic ideology allows ideology to continue exercising power and constraint on hailed subjects and it also hides relations of epistemic domination. Another approach is that ideology no longer relies upon interpellating individuals into subjects; instead neoliberal ideology offers a value-neutral mechanism represented by rights (Zizek, Living in the End Times 2011, 40).

The fact that the hailed subject practices the ideology's core principles, guarantees its long-lasting existence without the need for the use of direct force or repression. Ideology presents itself as something natural or inevitable, when in reality it is something socially and politically constructed. 'One of the effects of ideology is the practical denegation of the ideological character of ideology by ideology' (Althusser, On the Reproduction of Capitalism: Ideology and Ideological State Apparatuses 2014, 191). The naturalisation of the core principles of an ideology results in the effects and influence of an ideology becoming something invisible to the person interpellated by it and perceived instead as something obvious (Mudge 2008); 'what we cannot directly talk about can be shown by the form of our activity. What the official ideology cannot openly talk about may be revealed in the mute signs of a building' (Zizek, Living in the End Times 2011, 255).

Hailed individuals do not notice the effects, direct and indirect, that ideology has upon their relationships with the world. The naturalisation and invisibility to them of a particular form of ideology hides the effect that their unconscious devotion to it contributes to its maintenance and reproduction, making the situation natural, indispensable and beneficial (Althusser, On the Reproduction of Capitalism: Ideology and Ideological State Apparatuses 2014, 252). Education and training play a major role in the inculcation and spread of the hegemonic ideology.

In the process of understanding how ideology becomes part of individuals' daily lives, Susan Marks developed a much-elaborated theory of five principal modes and strategies of operation used by ideology. Those five modes and strategies are: 'legitimation, dissimulation, unification, reification and naturalization' (Marks 2003, 19).

As presented by Marks, '[l]egitimation is the process by which authority comes to seem valid and appropriate' (Marks 2003, 19). Dissimulation, is the process 'whereby relations of domination are obscured, masked or denied' (Marks 2003, 20). Ideology in this form dissimulates and obscures relationships of domination by using encrypted language. Unification, is the process 'in which social relations come to appear coherent and harmonious, and cleavages are made to seem non-existent, or, at any rate, irrelevant' (Marks 2003).

In addition, reification, 'refers to a process by which a human's products come to appear as if they were material things, and then to dominate those who produced them' (Marks 2003). The conditions of the world are no longer seen as a human construction but are, instead, perceived as unchangeable conditions in which the role of the individual is limited to that of an observer. In this form, relations of domination and/or inequality are seen as eternal, as if they had been always there, and nothing can be done in that regard. Finally, the last mode as presented by Marks is naturalisation, 'whereby existing social arrangements come to seem obvious and self-evident, as if they were natural phenomena belonging to a world "out there"' (Marks 2003, 22). In this way, what in reality is the result of historical processes such as colonialism is simply perceived as a natural condition.

Ideology determines the way in which individuals behave adopting certain lines of conduct and following certain practices and rituals (Althusser, On the Reproduction of Capitalism: Ideology and Ideological State Apparatuses 2014, 185). Hailed individuals, influence entities such as states, international organisations or multinational corporations (MNCs) which are associations made up of individuals.

In the specific case of neoliberalism as a form of ideology, it has permeated public and private institutions (domestically and internationally). Thus, it hails many individuals and determines the way in which they relate to the world, and determines their writings, speeches, personal relations, and in general, the agency of the individual in society (Heron 2008). Thus, even if IIL stakeholders (such as arbitrators) become aware, even for a fraction of second of the negative consequences of the system, the encroached neoliberal ideology guarantees that all will follow the herd so as to underpin IIL. It is within this scenario that it becomes very important to distinguish the reality as it appears to IIL stakeholders, hailed by the neoliberal ideology, compared to a reality seen from a different perspective by individuals that have not been subjectivised by the hegemonic ideology.

Chapter 5

THE RISE OF NEOLIBERALISM

To better understand neoliberalism as ideology, it is important to pursue a brief genealogical analysis of the rise of this particular form of ideology, its clashes and struggles, and specifically the triangular relationship between state, society and market. What follows is a general overview of relevant events in the construction and consolidation of neoliberalism.

One of the first antecedents was the 1934 publication of the Henry Simons pamphlet "A Positive Program for Laissez-faire" (Peck, Constructions of Neoliberal Reason 2012, 54). In this pamphlet, Simons defended the idea that the state needed to take an important and active role in maintaining competitive market conditions, including controlling currency fluctuation and protecting property rights, among others (Simons 1948). Later, in 1938, the Walter Lippmann Colloquium[2] was the ideal space to gather intellectuals from the United States and Western Europe, who shared common thoughts about the role of the state in the economy (Prieto-Rios, Neoliberal Market Rationality: The Driver of International Investment Law 2015). Among those participating in this colloquium were, Friedrich August Von Hayek, Ludwig von Mises, Raymond Aron, Milton Friedman, Jacques Rueff, Wilhelm Röpke and Alexander Rüstow. The colloquium celebrated the publication of Walter Lippmann's *The Good Society* in which Lipmann criticised collectivism and central planning (Turner 2007).

The attendees at Lippmann's colloquium used it as platform to promote within the Western world an updated form of liberalism, which was considered by many of the participants, to be an essential element in keeping western civilisation 'on track' (Turner 2007). It is claimed that it was during this colloquium that Alexander Rüstow coined the term 'neoliberalism' to describe the updated form of liberalism they wanted to promote (Turner 2007).

The discussions held at the Walter Colloquium (as well as in other academic spaces at the time) were the direct response to the collectivism and central planning that was swamping Europe during the first half of the twentieth century. It is important to remember that the Third Reich adopted a series of economic policies of which central planning, and excessive state control of the economy, including restricting the functioning of the market, were main characteristics (Neumann, Marcuse and Kirchheimer 2013).

In the same vein, intellectuals from the German Schools of Frankfurt and Freiburg also maintained a critical approach to economic policies of central planning promoted by the Nazi government in Germany. Critics of the

---

[2] The Lippmann Colloquium held in Paris in August 1938 organised by the French philosopher Louis Rougier and was named after the famed American journalist Walter Lippmann.

central planning model adopted by the Nazi government considered it to be fully based on Keynesian principles (Lapavistas 2005, 31-32). People such as Franz Neumann, Herbert Marcuse Otto Kircheimer, Friedrich Pollock, Walter Eucken, among others, became part of the anti-Nazi intellectual resistance (Neumann, Marcuse and Kirchheimer 2013). Newman and Kircheimer later worked as political analysts at the Office of Strategic Services (OSS)[3] – the first U.S. intelligence agency – in the Central European Section (Neumann, Marcuse and Kirchheimer 2013). They defended their collaboration with the USA as a way of putting their critical theory into practice against the Nazi government in Germany (Neumann, Marcuse and Kirchheimer 2013).

After the fall of the Nazi regime, and with the occupation of Germany by the Allies, the two schools of thought (Frankfurt and Freiburg) gained the recognition and support of occupation forces and of certain sectors of the German population as an academic alternative for the reconstruction of the German economy (Gerber 1994). Likewise, world-wide academic movements that defended the idea of limiting the role and activity of the state, whilst defending economic liberalism, so as to avoid another catastrophe, gained ground. Accordingly in 1948, just three years after the end of Second World War, Walter Eucken and Franz Böhm founded the *Journal Jahrbuchfür die Ordnung von Wirtschaf und Gesellschaft* (ORDO Journal n.d.), better known as the *Ordo Journal* (the foundation for the term 'ordoliberals') (M. Foucault, The Birth of Biopolitics: Lectures at the College De France, 1978–1979 2008, 109–110).

The term 'Ordoliberals' was used to refer to the group of academics writing in the Ordo journal that shared certain core principles, including favouring a relatively strong, but not expansive, state charged with maintaining a competitive environment with the objective of securing conditions of economic freedom (Peck, Constructions of Neoliberal Reason 2012). Another shared core principle was a direct criticism of pure forms of liberalism, as it was considered that problems arising out of laissez-faire policies generated the first steps towards a centrally planned state (Peck, Constructions of Neoliberal Reason 2012).

According to the Ordoliberals, the state must not intervene directly in the economy as its main role should focus on creating the right conditions for the market to function autonomously; this included the abolition of cartels and monopolies and protecting private property (Mudge 2008). Other relevant aspects proposed by the Ordoliberals included the creation of an economic constitution, the guarantee of private property, protection of economic

---

[3] The OSS was the forerunner of the CIA.

liberties, and in general, the elimination of any type of barrier or limitation to free commerce or free market competition (Gerber 1994).

In parallel with the German intellectual movement against central planning and Keynesian economics, a similar movement was taking place on the other side of the Atlantic at the University of Chicago. The early Chicago School, led by Henry Simons, was similar to the twentieth century Manchesterian and Austrian Laissez-faire that argued for a full autonomous and free market (Peck, Constructions of Neoliberal Reason 2012, 17). However, the post-war Chicago School led by Milton Friedman took a more radical approach towards the state, the market and the relationship between both, by combining anti-statism with pro-free market (Peck, Constructions of Neoliberal Reason 2012).

In 1953 Friedman in his essay in 'Positive Economics' emphasised the difference between normative economics (what ought to be) and positivist economics (what is), giving priority to the latter, as it offers more certainty in analysis (Mäki 2009). The use of the mathematics as 'neutral' language played an important role in the expansion of the neoclassical economic discourse, which forms an essential part of neoliberalism (Peck, Constructions of Neoliberal Reason 2012, 63). Chicago also favoured a market logic in which 'private and voluntary' were prioritised over 'public and mandatory' (Peck, Remaking laissez-faire 2008).

A third important school of economic thought in the consolidation, of what is known as neoliberalism and which tends to be ignored, was the twentieth century Spanish Economic School of thought, that characterised by a mixture of anti-Keynesianism combined with economic theology (Guardiola-Rivera, Story of a Death Foretold: The Coup Against Salvador Allende, 11 September 1973 2013, 183). This school of thought was inspired by the study of the economic ideas of the Jesuit School of Salamanca of the sixteenth and seventeenth century, Christian theology, and ideas of St Thomas Aquinas (Guardiola-Rivera, Story of a Death Foretold: The Coup Against Salvador Allende, 11 September 1973 2013, 185). Specifically, the Jesuit School of Salamanca argued that it was a Christian duty to rebel against a government that limited the liberty of individuals and their associations, regardless of whether the interventions implied redistributive measures (Guardiola-Rivera, Story of a Death Foretold: The Coup Against Salvador Allende, 11 September 1973 2013, 185–189).

According to the Spanish Economic School of thought, the state had the duty of not interfering with the liberty of individuals (Guardiola-Rivera, Story of a Death Foretold: The Coup Against Salvador Allende, 11 September 1973 2013, 185). This school of thought was the result of a combination of medieval Catholic principles of the autonomy and freedom of guilds, combined with a liberal-individualistic economic stance against Keynesianism

(Guardiola-Rivera, Story of a Death Foretold: The Coup Against Salvador Allende, 11 September 1973 2013, 158). Members of this School include theologians such as Aniceto de Castro Albarrán, Juan Vasquez de Mella, Salvador Millet i Bel, Juan Sardá, Gonzalo Fernandez de la Mora, Rafael Calvo Serer and Lucas Beltran (Beltran was a constant attendee at the annual meetings of the MPS and LSE alumni) (Schwartz 1997).

It is important to highlight that the Spaniards have had contact with Erhards's ideas back in the 1940s (Guardiola-Rivera, Story of a Death Foretold: The Coup Against Salvador Allende, 11 September 1973 2013). Later in 1949, Hayek visited Madrid and Barcelona where he met with Salvador Millet I Bel, Jordan Sardaa and Lucas Beltran (Guardiola-Rivera, Story of a Death Foretold: The Coup Against Salvador Allende, 11 September 1973 2013, 185). It is noteworthy that the 1959 Stabilization Plan, designed by Juan Sardá to reform Spain's economy during the final part of the Franco era, was influenced by the Mont Pèlerin Society, the Freiburg School and the Spanish Economic School of thought. In turn, it would become quite influential in the Americas, especially among young students in conservative Catholic institutions and particularly so in Chile during the 1960s and 1970s (Sánchez Lissen 2005).

It was in this context of transatlantic movements against central planning and Keynesianism, that the Austrian Economist Friedrich August von Hayek played an important role in providing a bridge for transatlantic conversations between Ordoliberals, Chicagoans and the Spanish Economic School of thought. It is important to highlight that despite some clear and marked differences among Chicago, the Ordoliberals and the Spaniards, all positions took a common view of rejecting Keynesianism, Socialism and central planning.

One of the most relevant and important texts written by Hayek was the 'Road to Serfdom' published months prior to the end of the Second World War. Its main arguments focused on a frontal attack against socialism and central planning, which for him constituted the first steps towards totalitarianism and tyranny (Peck, Constructions of Neoliberal Reason 2012, 47). Hayek argued not for a radical laissez-faire, but for the need of promoting competition and creating the legal conditions for such competition to happen. However, as highlighted by Keynes, Hayek failed to indicate the role of the state in the dialectics between the legal framework and the free functioning of the market (Peck, Constructions of Neoliberal Reason 2012, 48).

As a result of Hayek's liking for the Alps, he organised an international conference, which gathered pro-liberals and anti-collectivists at the Mont Pelerin Resort in 1947. This meeting was the first meeting of the Mont Pelerin Society (MPS) which was in a certain form the continuation of the meeting previously held in Paris in 1938 (Turner 2007). The meeting allowed Hayek to bring together liberal economic thinkers from Austria, Germany, Britain,

Spain and the USA (Birch and Mykhnenko, A World Turned Right Way Up 2010). All the attendees agreed on the need to 'reconstruct liberal philosophy' in an era of central planning (Butler n.d.) (Hayek 1947).

Among different MPS aims was the redefinition of the role of the state, the need to create a global order to create an international economic agreement (Birch and Mykhnenko, A World Turned Right Way Up 2010), and the strong defence of competition, and property regimes (Turner 2007). A statement issued by the MPS about the aims of the society expressed the following:

> Over large stretches of the earth's surface the essential conditions of human dignity and freedom have already disappeared. In others, they are under constant menace from the development of current tendencies of policy. The position of the individual and the voluntary groups are progressively under-mined by the extension of arbitrary power…The group believes that these developments have been fostered by the growth of a view of history which denies all absolute moral standards and by the growth of theories which question the desirability of the rule of law. It holds further that they have been fostered by the decline of belief in private property and the competitive market; for without the diffused power and initiative associated with these institutions it is difficult to imagine a society in which freedom may be effectively preserved. (Turner 2007)

The MPS became the place for transatlantic conversation, creating bridges between the Ordoliberals in Central Europe and Spain as well as the Chicagoans from the USA. The society also created space for conversations among academics, politicians and businessmen. The role of the MPS was essential to crafting neoliberalism as a flexible ideological project with different approaches and different perspectives but with some unchangeable core of principles (Peck, Constructions of Neoliberal Reason 2012, 66).

The strategy of the MPS was to persuade global intellectuals and economic leaders about the benefits and importance of neoliberal ideology and the negative effects of Keynesianism (Miller 2010). Business and wealthy economic sponsors (who were also friends of the MPS) helped in its worldwide expansion, specifically supporting the creation of think-tanks set up to promote neoliberal ideology (Birch and Mykhnenko, A World Turned Right Way Up 2010).

Many MPS members attained important positions in countries such as Germany, Italy, Francoist Spain, Chile, the USA, the United Kingdom, among others (Peck, Constructions of Neoliberal Reason 2012, 51). The first major MPS victory was the monetary policy adopted in Western Germany in 1948. Ludwig Erhard (who was also an MPS member) acting Finance Minister launched a plan for the Deutsche Mark together with deregulation in certain areas (Peck, Constructions of Neoliberal Reason 2012). In the same sense, another victory (seen over the long term) was the signing of the first Bilateral Investment Treaty (BIT) with Pakistan.

Different members of the MPS dedicated their lives to the promotion of its principles in various locations around the world, from Chile to China, and passing through the USA and the United Kingdom. Such is the case of Antony Fisher, who dedicated his life in the United Kingdom, as well as in the United States, to the promotion of free market policies and neoliberal ideas whilst opening think tanks in London and New York. Fisher founded the Institute of Economic Affairs in London in 1955 (Blundell 2015); later in November 1977, with the Support of Wall Street Financer William Casey, Fisher founded the International Centre for Economic Policy Studies in New York (Frost 2008), (rebranded as the Manhattan Institute for Policy Research) (Manhattan Forums n.d.). Fisher also founded the Atlas Economic Research Foundation in San Francisco in 1981 for the promotion of free market, liberal thinking and the protection of private property (Atlas Economic Research Foundation n.d.). Atlas contributed to the formation of free-market neoliberal think tanks in different countries, including among others Peru, Argentina, Chile, Turkey and Lithuania (Atlas Economic Research Foundation n.d.). Fisher, speaking about an encounter with, and advice given by, Hayek related the following:

> Hayek first warned me against wasting time – as I was then tempted – by taking up a political career. He explained his view that the decisive influence in the battle of ideas and policy was wielded by intellectuals whom he characterised as the second-hand dealers in ideas. It was the dominant intellectuals from the Fabians[4] onwards who had tilted the political debate in favour of growing government intervention with all that followed. If I shared the view that better ideas were not getting a fair hearing, his counsel was that I should join with others in forming a scholarly research organisation to supply intellectuals in universities, schools, journalism and broadcasting with authoritative studies of the economic theory of markets and its application to practical affairs. (Fisher 1978, 79–80)

On the road to positioning neoliberal ideology upfront on the world scene, Washington Consensus institutions also played a key role in its expansion. It is important to explain that the term 'Washington Consensus' was coined by the economist John Williamson who identified common patterns in the imposition of politics by the International Monetary Fund (IMF), the World Bank and the Federal Reserve upon Latin America. The reforms proposed

---

[4] Fabians – founded 1884 by Beatrice and Sidney Webb, George Bernard Shaw, and H. G. Wells as a group promoting non-Marxist revolutionary socialism.

by the Washington Consensus reflected core neoliberal principles promoted by the MPS and the Chicago School. Some of the principles included market liberalisation, an end to subsidies, a strong property system, a favourable environment for foreign investment, privatisation, among other things (Birch and Mykhnenko, A World Turned Right Way Up 2010).

IMF and World Bank technocrats promoted a discourse according to which countries should embrace free trade and become attractive for foreign investors, because the combination of both would promote economic growth and development. The IMF and the World Bank, used their lending power to impose a neoliberal agenda in recipient countries mainly from the global south (Elisa Van Wayenberge n.d.).

The World Bank used the famous Structural Adjustment Programs (SAPS), aimed at ensuring debt repayment by Latin American Countries, to impose a clear neoliberal agenda. SAPS conditioned countries to programmes of liberalisation, privatisation, a favourable environment for foreign investors and stability at the macroeconomic level (Stiglitz 1999). After long internal and external criticisms, the Bank changed SAPS for Performance Based Allocation (PBA) programmes (Elisa Van Wayenberge n.d.). Under the scenarios of PBAs, the Bank assesses whether the conditions of the country met its internal policies before giving 'aid towards development' to the requesting country (Elisa Van Wayenberge n.d.).

As presented in this section, by the 1970s and 1980s, many individuals in countries and institutions having a global reach, had been hailed by a growing and stronger ideology: neoliberalism. Moreover, those hailed individuals, as did others in think tanks, schools, universities and governments contributed to the expansion of neoliberal ideology. They transformed it into a hegemonic way of viewing and relating to the world and evolving within it. Thirty years of arduous work paid off by making neoliberal ideology unstoppable; it started with Henry Simons' pamphlet "A Positive Program for Laissez-Faire" and continues today with the Big Society of former British Prime Minister David Cameron and Donald Trump´s market defence of USA companies world-wide under the banner of Make America Great Again.

IIL AND THE NEOLIBERAL IDEOLOGY

Neoliberalism as the dominant hegemonic ideology since 1970s has exercised a profound influence on the IIL system by offering an 'operating framework or ideological software for this international legal system' (Peck and Tickell, Neoliberalizing Space 2002). Specifically, the IIL system, provided fertile soil for the implementation of neoliberal core principles as well as an ideal vehicle for the expansion of neoliberal ideology. In fact, the 1980s marked the moment in which International Economic Law (IEL), of which IIL is a sub-branch, became the most important field of international law as confirmed by its scope, volume and efficiency (Faundez and Tan 2010). IIL as part of IEL fully reflects the Washington Consensus and became one of the main instruments for the transformation of Washington Consensus principles into binding norms (Faundez and Tan 2010).

To a greater degree than in other agreements, IIAs include clauses that reproduce neoliberal core principles. These principles have provided either the connecting dots between an expanding ideology and the IIL system or the basis for re-shaping the system in accordance with the new hegemonic ideology. Those clauses include fair and equitable treatment clauses (FET), protection against indirect expropriation, promotion and the protection of investments. Perhaps among the most important is investment arbitration as a dispute settlement mechanism, which has been explained in detail in previous chapters. In this regard, Sonarajah mentions the following:

> For some of the developing countries that adopted neo-liberal policies, the consequences have been disastrous and have resulted in spectacularly failed economies. In the field of the law on foreign investment, the failure had left indelible results. In pursuance of the adoption of neo-liberal policies, Argentina had discarded the Calvo doctrine (despite espousing it for nearly a century) and had signed several investment treaties including one with the US. These policies led to an economic crisis and resulted in the need to take measures such as exchange controls and devaluation, which affected foreign investors. These measures also resulted in 46 claims for investment treaty violations, involving billions of dollars. (M. Sornarajah, Mutations of Neo-Liberalism in International Investment Law 2011)

From a neoliberal perspective, private property is regarded as an element essential to guarantee the spontaneous order of the market. According to this line of argument, private property and the protection of contractual relations offer the subject a feeling of trust and independence, thus allowing her to participate as an entrepreneur in the market (Turner 2007). The sanctity of property stands very high within the IIL system as it is protected against host state actions that could affect its full use and enjoyment. In this sense, expropriations, or limitations of private property are seen as actions that affect the liberty of the subject, weakening their ability to access and interact in the market (Turner 2007).

As already discussed in previous chapters, ISDS allows foreign investors to challenge any regulatory decision adopted by any authority in the host state bringing a claim against the host state before an International Investment

Arbitral Tribunal.[5] Investment Tribunals review decisions adopted by authorities of a sovereign state in compliance with their legal and constitutional duties (Elkins, Guzman and Simmons 2006).

In other words, the tribunal assesses the actions adopted by the host state against the terms and obligations agreed to in the international treaty. In this sense, the arbitral clause places investors and states on an equal footing, giving foreign investors the same *locus standi* as states, thus treating them as subjects of public international law. In this regard, Rene Urueña states the following:

> In those terms, the investor is a perfect example of the *homo economicous*: a subject of law whose very existence is tied to rational benefit maximizing activity. If the 'investor' fails to prove that she has undertaken an investment, then that actor will not be considered a subject of international investment law anymore. (Urueña 2012, 83)

The entitlement granted to the foreign investor to challenge the host state, contrasts with the limitations in place for interested third parties to participate and to be heard during the arbitral procedure (Prieto-Rios and Rivas, Neocolonialism and the Tension between International Investment Law and Indigenous Peoples: The Latin American Experience 2020). It is important to consider that on many occasions, the issues alleged by the investor relate to situations in which specific individuals or communities have been or could have been affected. The denial of *locus standi* to communities or individuals is an indication that the procedural structure prioritises the market and entrepreneurs above communities.

It is relevant to acknowledge that some countries, aware of the neoliberal influence in the IIL system, have attempted to oppose the IIL system, and seek changes in the entire system. For example, it is possible to find some Andean countries such Venezuela or Bolivia that have denounced the International Centre for Settlement of Investment Disputes (ICSID) convention or, in the case of Ecuador, that appointed a special commission to re-assess its Bilateral Investment Treaties (BITs). Furthermore, the Comprehensive Economic and Trade Agreement (CETA) between the EU and Canada, the Transatlantic Trade and Investment Partnership (TTIP) and the ongoing negotiations to

---

[5] According to the terms of the treaty (either BIT or FTA), any investor could request the composition of an arbitral tribunal to resolve a dispute with the host state. The claim could be resolved either by an ad hoc tribunal or an institutional tribunal. The ad hoc tribunal acts independently of any international institution and depends entirely upon the regulations agreed by the parties. On the other hand, the institutional tribunal is linked to organisations which specialise in the matter of arbitral procedures; the most common for that purpose being the International Centre for Settlement of Investment Disputes (ICSID) and the International Chamber of Commerce (ICC).

reform ICSID comprise a part of some responses from the system to the different criticisms.⁶ These initiatives such as CETA will be analysed more specifically in the next chapter.

CONCLUSION

As argued in this chapter, neoliberalism has moved from being an ideology sitting along the side-lines to become the new common sense. It hails individuals and has become a globalised and hegemonic rationalisation for global economics, IIL and state reforms (Peck and Tickell, Neoliberalizing Space 2002). Ideology can generally be understood as a system of dominating ideas and representations which has a material experience that affects the material world, and in the process, also affects social reproduction (Althusser, Lenin and Philosophy and Other Essays 1971, 297). In this sense, the system of ideas and representations has a real effect on the way subjects experience the world.

Part of the world-wide success of the neoliberal ideology project was its expansion beyond the economic realm into other domains, permeating not only the market but also all institutional apparatuses and all the different areas including education, law, government, politics, the economy, among others (Brown 2005, 37–38). Neoliberal ideology defends the limitation of state intervention in the economy (the state oversees the functioning of the market but does not intervene), privatisation, reduction of social investments and promotion of entrepreneurs and extreme protection of property rights among others (De Sousa Santos 2002, 314).

The ideology is enforced by global institutions, local technocrats and elites who seem to be in charge of policing compliance with the core of the strategy (Peck and Tickell, Neoliberalizing Space 2002). As shown in this chapter, the victory of neoliberalism was not something natural but rather the direct result of almost thirty years of hard work, fighting in the field of ideas and ideology (Peck and Tickell, Neoliberalizing Space 2002). Neoliberalism has become the only legitimate model of modernity.

Neoliberal ideology is characterised by its plasticity which has allowed it to be applied, with rigidity or flexibility where necessary, offering solutions to problems. Regardless of the speciality or social context, it accommodates itself to the realities of each moment, offering comprehensive and united

---

⁶ It is important to mention that although these so-called 'new treaties' attempt to respond to criticisms the modifications are mild and the system and the core (?) protection offered to the foreign investor does not change substantially leaving the IIL system intact.

answers to problems, whilst maintaining the same core principles (Peck and Tickell, Neoliberalizing Space 2002).

Neoliberal ideology has also shaped the IIL system in the sense of maintaining and reproducing unfair and unbalanced relations of economic and legal control on a global scale. The investment system combines the protection of private property, promotion of foreign investments, related in many cases to processes of privatisation, with the limitation of the State's capacity to regulate.

IIL system is in place to protect foreign investors regardless of issues of public interests such as human rights, environmental protection and labour standards (M. Sornarajah, Mutations of Neo-Liberalism in International Investment Law 2011). In this sense, it is important to think about the possibilities of emancipatory change looking beyond neoliberalism. Perhaps to find such alternatives, we will have to look at Latin American countries such as Ecuador or Bolivia that are working on different alternatives, moving 'towards a new common sense' in how one views and interacts with the world.

Chapter 6

IIL: An Autopoietic System

The conception of a self-generating legal system is as familiar to common lawyers as it is bizarre to lawyers trained in the Continental traditions of positivism and naturalism. (Jacobson 1989, 1678)

INTRODUCTION

In the previous chapter, I analysed neoliberalism as the core ideology behind the functioning of the International Investment Law (IIL) system. I argued that it serves to hide situations of systemic violence created by the IIL system. Nonetheless, despite the naturalisation of the system by some subjects, the system has still been under heavy criticism by non-interpellated individuals who have identified its harmful effects. Hence, in this last chapter, I argue that some important changes within the IIL, specifically to the Investor State Dispute Settlement (ISDS) procedure, which came in response to various of the criticisms, and which have been hailed as positive, are nothing more than actions adopted by the system itself to continue its existence and as such perpetuating itself.

In order to develop this argument, I use the analytical tool of autopoiesis (following Niklas Luhman) to analyse the operation of the IIL as a self-contained system that re-enacts and perpetuates itself. A system is autopoietic when it 'reproduces its own elements through their interaction' (Rottleuthner 1988, 114). Using autopoiesis as unit of analysis, allows us to understand the independence and autonomy of the IIL system. It is in this way that the IIL system generates its own legal materials out of its own functioning and validates itself.

As has been previously discussed in this book, the IIL is a system in the sense that it consists of arrangement of elements that correlate one to another; they cannot be understood as isolated elements (Zarra 2018). The system has evolved from being a simple set of rules for the regulation of the states' activities in regards to foreign investors, to becoming as well an instrument of global governance for the discipline of states. It provides a structure for truly global social orders (Schill 2009, 1), which has direct implications about how people are governed around the world (Harten, Sovereign Choices and Sovereign Constraints 2013) and, as such, facilitates situations of systemic violence.

As developed in earlier chapters, one of the main challenges and criticisms has been that the Investor State Dispute Settlement (ISDS) system allows off shore Arbitral Tribunals to decide the international legality or illegality of sovereign acts (acts *jure imperii*) adopted by legislative, judicial or administrative bodies. The powers granted to Arbitral Tribunals are broad enough that they have the ability to review acts and decisions of democratically elected bodies (Harten, Sovereign Choices and Sovereign Constraints 2013). Furthermore, there are the facts that the system does not include any appeal body, and that transparency and issues of conflict of interests usually give rise to distrust from the outside about the functioning of IIL and, specifically, of ISDS.

Another important criticism of the ISDS is that the amount of money awarded as reparation for the commission of an internationally wrongful act could generate strains upon host states, and in particular for developing countries. For instance, for the period 1996–2017, the claims of foreign investors against Latin American countries amounted to USD$145,8 billion and the amount of money that states have been ordered to pay as compensation was of USD$20.6 billion (Olivet, Müller and Ghiotto 2017). Two examples are the cases of *Occidental v Ecuador*, in which the Tribunal initially ordered the state to pay the sum of USD$2,3 billion, later reduced to USD$1,061 billion (*Occidental Petroleum Corporation and Occidental Exploration and Production Company v. The Republic of Ecuador* 2012) and the case of *Mobil et al v Venezuela*, in which the tribunal ordered the state to pay USD$1.6 billion to the foreign investor (Venezuela Holdings, B.V., et al (case formerly known as Mobil Corporation, Venezuela Holdings, B.V., et al.) v. Bolivarian Republic of Venezuela 2014).

It is in this context that the common understanding that IIL requires certain changes to respond to the mounting criticisms, has gained importance among decision-making interpreters (initiated). This idea is reflected by all the different initiatives to modify the ISDS regime. For example, ICSID and UNCITRAL procedures are undergoing certain reforms, so too are the different models of Bilateral Investments Treaties (BITs) developed by countries, which changes are characterised by increasing protection for the regulatory activity of the state. It is also important to highlight that, in the same vein, some Arbitral Tribunals have broadened their scopes of analysis at the moment of assessing a foreign investor´s claim, thus opening the door to other International Law´s regimes. In the following sections, I will analyse some of the most relevant initiatives changes within the ISDS procedure.

ISDS: BETWEEN BLURB AND DARK

Before the 2000s, ISDS was generally unknown and misunderstood, not only by people in general, but even for those involved in the negotiation of International Investment Agreements (IIA). It was not until the late 1990s that claims under the North Atlantic Free Trade Agreement (NAFTA) umbrella brought to public attention the bearing that ISDS could have on the ability of host states to regulate and its impact on local communities (Harten, Investment Treaty Arbitration and Public Law 2007). The number of investment arbitration procedures increased considerably during the late 1990s and early 2000s. According to the UNCTAD, between 1987 and 1998, only 14 investment treaty disputes had been brought before the ICSID, while in 2006 this number had risen to 259 (United Nations Conference on Trade and Development 2007, 7). The increase in the number of arbitration cases has attracted criticism from different sides of the spectrum mainly because '(it) is perceived as non-responsive to the necessities of a form of adjudication that involves strong features of public law' meaning that the system is perceived as alien to proper assessment of sovereign state decisions (Zarra 2018). Other criticism, and as notes in chapter 4, is the encryption of the system that makes it not only difficult for outsiders to understand but also makes it difficult for policy makers to foresee the outcome of their actions (Prieto-Rios, Encrypted International Investment Law in the Age of Neo-Colonialism 2018).

Investment Tribunals are created and limited by the consent of two or more states represented in an IIA. Such Tribunals have the duty and the right to interpret the treaty and give meaning to its terms while not exceeding the jurisdiction granted by the treaty[1] (Schill 2009). In this sense, ISDS, as a mechanism to resolve conflicts between investors and the host states, is

---

[1] In the context of ISDS, the terms 'competence' and 'jurisdiction' are frequently used interchangeably. This despite the fact that both are included in the ICSID Convention and the ICSID Arbitration Rules. It can be stated that jurisdiction is an abstract and general concept that in ICSID Arbitration refers to the jurisdiction of the Center, while competence is a more specific concept that refers to the competence of the tribunal over a particular case. As such, the tribunal has competence, and the Center has jurisdiction. If there is competence, there is jurisdiction, yet if there is jurisdiction, there is not necessarily competence (Heiskanen 2014):

exceptional within Public International Law taking into consideration that (i) Multinational Corporations (MNCs) when protected by an IIA are entitled to challenge the legality of acts *jure imperii* and not only acts *jure gestionis*; (ii) in the majority of cases, according to the IIAs wording, investors are not required to exhaust domestic remedies; (iii) cases are not resolved by a unique or a permanent international tribunal; (iv) so far, IIA only impose obligations to the host states and upon to the foreign investors.

The fact that these non-permanent arbitral tribunals assess the legality of acts *jure imperii* and not only acts *jure gestionis* has attracted different criticisms. For instance, Gus Van Harten sates the following:

> Thus, it appeared unexceptional for arbitrators to review democratically-accountable decisions taken on behalf of a population and to decide whether public compensation was warranted for an affected foreign asset owner. By implication, a core element of the authority of states – the supremacy of their legislative power – clearly has been altered by investment treaties. (Harten, Sovereign Choices and Sovereign Constrains 2013, 52)

As it was briefly mentioned in chapter 3 of this book, arbitral tribunals, at the moment of analysing the legality of the acts of the state, have followed two main approaches. On the one hand, arbitral tribunals have adopted the 'sole effect doctrine', that is analysing the sole effects of the measure adopted by the host state on the rights of the foreign investor protected by an IIA (Peter D. Isakoff 2013). For instance, in the case *Metalclad v Mexico,* the analysis of the tribunal focused on whether the measures adopted by the Mexican state violated the NAFTA protection against indirect expropriation, without considering arguments related to environmental protection (*Metalclad Corporation v. The United Mexican States* 2000). Also, in the case, *Santa Helena v Costa Rica* the tribunal did not consider the environmental reasons considered by the Costa Rican government and concluded that the measure amounted to an indirect expropriation protected by the Bilateral Investment Treaty (BIT) (*Compañia del Desarrollo de Santa Elena S.A. v. Republic of Costa Rica 2000*).

This restricted approach has placed limitations upon tribunals to accept human rights arguments, and turned it into a form of self-contained system. Regarding self-contained systems, the International Law Commission (ILC) has stated the following:

> Thus, provisionally, it is possible to distinguish between two uses for the notion of 'self-contained regime'. In a narrow sense, the term is used to denote a special set of secondary rules under the law of State responsibility that claims primacy to the general rules concerning consequences of a violation. In a broader

sense, the term is used to refer to interrelated wholes of primary and secondary rules, sometimes also referred to as 'systems' or 'subsystems' of rules that cover some particular problem differently from the way it would be covered under general law. (Koskenniemi 2006)

Nonetheless, the approach that IIL is a self-contained system has been criticised by different scholars. For instance, Zarra has expressed his doubts on asserting that IIL is a self-contained system considering that investment tribunals refer to sources of Public International Law (PIL) as well as taking into consideration other of its branches (Zarra 2018).

On the other hand, some tribunals have taken the 'police power doctrine' approach. Accordingly, tribunals take into consideration the context, the purpose and the nature of the measures adopted by the host state, not limited to comparing the facts and the effects of the measure against the text of the IIA. For instance, in the case *Saluka Investment v Czech Republic* the tribunal took into consideration the police powers and the regulatory capacity of the host state. In this case, the tribunal concluded that the measures adopted by the government to protect the financial system were part of its regulatory capacity (*Saluka Investments B.V. v. The Czech Republic* 2005).

Another major challenge faced by the IIL system and its stakeholders, especially states, has been the lack of coherence of the awards. This makes it difficult to foresee whether a decision adopted by any authority within host state could amount to a breach of an international obligation contained within an IIA. This situation has been the result of the non-existence of one single international tribunal to resolve disputes between foreign investors and host states. There are, in addition, the realities that in International Law in general, but specifically in IIL, there is no 'binding' precedent and the fact that IIL is an encrypted system.

It is important to remember that, in International Law, precedent does not exist, as it would violate the voluntarist approach. Hence, '[i]f decisions were binding beyond the individual case, States would lose their exclusive position as the creators of international law' (Schill 2009, 282–283). Nonetheless, there is an inter-awards dialogue between various and different tribunals that could lead to the conclusion that there is an ongoing construction of a *jurisprudence constante* or persistent jurisprudence. This is an expression that has been adopted to describe situations in which tribunals, despite the absence of binding precedent, refer to previous well-reasoned decisions of tribunals that interpreted and applied identical or similar treaty provisions in a persuasive manner (Bjorklund 2008).

In the case of the encryption of the system, beyond the arguments put forward in chapter 4 of this book, it is also important to highlight that tribunals frequently draw conclusions from wholly or partly unrelated third-party BITs and also make reference to model treaties (Schill, The Multilateralization of International Investment Law 2009, 294, 312). For instance, this happened in the annulment of the decisions of *Compañia de Aguas del Aconquija v Argentina* in which the tribunal used the NAFTA, an unrelated IIA, to support its interpretation. Another example is the case of *Plama v Bulgaria* in which the Tribunal used a BIT with the United Kingdom to support its interpretation. In the case *Tokios Tokelés v Ukraine,* the Tribunal used the United States – Argentina BIT to support its interpretation. In the case *Enron v Argentina* and *El Paso v Argentina* the Tribunals used the U.S. model investment treaty at the moment of interpreting the facts of the case.

The difficulties faced by IIL stakeholders, but especially host states, for the lack of clarity surrounding the ISDS has reinforced criticisms from politicians, NGOs and academics. For instance, Cecilia Malmström in 2015, European Commissioner for Trade, stated the following:

> From the start of my mandate almost a year ago, ISDS has been one of the most controversial issues in my brief. I met and listened to many people and organisations, including NGOs, which voiced a number of concerns about the old, traditional system. It's clear to me that all these complaints had one common feature – that there is a fundamental and widespread lack of trust by the public in the fairness and impartiality of the old ISDS model. This has significantly affected the public's acceptance of ISDS and of companies bringing such cases. (Malmström 2015)

As a response to the broad criticisms towards the IIL system and the ISDS, certain awards have opened the door for a more comprehensive analysis of the situations faced by host states and have also opened the door for human rights and environmental arguments to be considered. Furthermore, the International Centre for Settlement of Investment Disputes (ICSID) and the United Nations Commission on International Trade Law (UNCITRAL) arbitral procedures have undergone reform discussions. In addition, countries have promoted model IIAs as an attempt to limit the lack of clarity and the broad powers given to arbitral tribunals.

ISDS: OPEN TO REFORMS?

As noted in the previous section, ISDS has been criticised by different IIL system stakeholders, not only located in the Global South but also in the Global North. This provides the context within which different proposals for fashioning substantial changes to ISDS have been put forward. These proposals explore means of reforming the system focusing mainly on changes to the ISDS (Zarra 2018). For instance, the European Union (EU) has made proposals for a Multilateral Investment Court of Arbitration (MIC) (European Commission 2016) and academics have proposed the inclusion of an appellate mechanism for arbitral awards (Bottini 2016). Another proposal includes the creation of a permanent arbitration court to create balance for the lack of permanence and the conflicts of interest encountered by investment arbitrators (Harten 2008; Langford, Behn and Lie 2017). Other proposed reforms have focused on reforming existing institutional and *ad hoc* arbitral procedures, specifically ICSID and UNCITRAL, and the development of new generations of model BITs.

The first set of changes that have materialised as a direct response to the criticisms and to the different proposals are the ongoing ICSID (institutional arbitration) and UNCITRAL's (ad hoc arbitration) discussions for reforms. The ongoing discussions are direct responses to criticism related to funding transparency, arbitrators' conflicts of interests and the appeal option, among others. I present below an overview of the ongoing reforms to those two arbitral procedures.

There have been ongoing discussions, since 2016, to reform ICSID and the ICSID Additional Facility Rules. In this context, four working papers have been published reflecting on different aspects that need to be reformed (ICSID 2018; International Institute for Sustainable Development 2019; ICSID 2020). These four papers have been shared with state members for their views on the proposed changes to the ICSID system but, to date, no final decision has been reached (ICSID 2020).

One aspect considered for reform is the disclosure of third-party funding, which can be described as 'the financing by a third party of a part or all of the costs of the arbitral proceeding for one of the parties to the dispute' (De Brabandere and Lepeltak 2012, 381) with the purpose of receiving a certain percentage of the compensation awarded to the funded party. This aspect raises critical issues related to the negative influence that third-party funders may have on the proceedings – obstructing, for example efforts to attain an amicable settlement – to the allocation of costs by tribunals and more generally to their impacts on the transparency of proceedings (Dautaj and Shirlow 2020). Garcia further argues that third-party funding 'is nothing else than a deliberate exploitation of the flaws in the BIT system for the benefit of speculators and at the cost of already-burdened respondent states, their taxpayers and citizens' (Garcia 2018, 2923).

Another aspect related to ICSID reform is the disclosure of the financial status of a requesting party and the corporate structure of a requesting party that is a legal entity (Dautaj and Shirlow 2020). The working papers also include reforms in terms of transparency of documents, hearings and deliberations (Dautaj and Shirlow 2020), whose existing rules have been framed based upon rules of international *commercial* arbitration that 'are not comparable to a fully public system of adjudication' (Langford, Potestà et al. 2020, 184), to which ISDS most resembles.

Along these lines, an UNCITRAL Working Group has been, since 2017, mandated to discuss multilateral options for its reform (International Institute for Sustainable Development 2017). Some of the issues on which the deliberation process has focused are 'excessive costs and lengthy proceedings, inconsistent and incorrect decisions, and a lack of arbitral diversity and independence' (Langford, Potestà et al. 2020, 167). Most reform options can be grouped into four categories: (i) improvement of ISDS, (ii) creation of an appellate mechanism, (iii) creation of a multilateral investment court and (iv) rejection altogether of ISDS in favour either of domestic courts or state-state arbitration (Langford, Potestà et al. 2020, 176). Some proposals include a code of conduct for third-party funders, reforms to the appointment of adjudicators, the establishment of an Advisory Centre on International Investment Law, and a code of conduct for arbitrators and judges (Langford, UNCITRAL and Investment Arbitration Reform: A Little More Action 2019; United Nations Commission on International Trade Law 2019; United Nations Commission on International Trade Law 2020).

The second set of changes that have responded to the criticisms and to the different proposals promoted by IIL stakeholders are the development of Model BITs that narrow the scope of interpretation of Investment Arbitral Tribunals by clarifying certain clauses. From 2004 onwards, developed and developing countries began a drafting process for Model BITs that included the protection of the regulatory activity of the state and suggested certain limits on the interpretation of the treaties by arbitral tribunals (Houde 2006). For instance, in the case of Canada, the country promoted Model BITs in 2004 and 2012. In the case of the 2012 model, among the relevant changes is included an updated form of the Hull formula of 'prompt, adequate and effective compensation' to the fair market value (following a similar NAFTA´s wording). The 2012 model also includes a clause encouraging states to promote standards of corporate social responsibility in their practices and internal policies. The model also includes a chapeau that protects the regulatory capacity of the states (Titi 2013) (Willard and Morreau 2015). It is important to point to the fact that Canada has recently opened opportunities for citizens to participate in 'how to make its foreign investment promotion and protection agreements (FIPAs) more inclusive and progressive' (Global Affairs Canada 2018).

Another relevant model is the 2012 USA Model BIT promoted by President Barack Obama. This document has been praised for incorporating important changes that benefit investors and host states (Office of the United States Trade Representative 2012). The aim of this treaty was to ensure that the public interest and the economic agenda of the country were reflected in the text (Office of the Spokesperson US Department of State 2012). The main changes to the treaty included promotion of transparency, the opportunity for state-parties to constantly review the treaties, and agree upon changes if necessary. The model also opened the possibility of a future appellate mechanism and included an obligation to not waive environmental and labour regulations (Office of the Spokesperson US Department of State 2012). The Model BIT also narrowed the scope of what is understood by the term 'investment'; explained more clearly the term 'minimum standard of treatment', included language to protect the regulatory capacity of host states regarding financial services and included a statute of limitations for the ISDS claims (Johnson 2012).

Two more relevant examples are the 2016 Indian Model BIT and the 2017 Colombia Model BIT. In the case of India, its 2016 Model BIT came as result of a flood of investment claims against the Indian government (Söderman 2020). This model 'does not include the most common BIT provision related to the international minimum standard. The text also restricts access to international arbitration, thus indicating a re-awakening of the Calvo doctrine and legal nationalism' (Söderman 2020). This Model BIT has been criticised for an extreme tilting of the balance in favour of the host state and for not taking into consideration the needs and concerns of foreign investors (Ranjan and Anand 2017).

The latter example relates to the process undertaken by Colombia starting in 2011 to develop a Model BIT that sets a balance between the interests of foreign investors and the sovereign regulatory capacity of the state (Prieto-Rios and Urueña, Colombia: un Estado bipolar en materia de inversión extranjera 2017). As a result of this process, which included public consultations, the Colombian government came up with the 2017 Model BIT (MINCIT (Colombian Ministry of Industry, Commerce and Tourism) 2017). On jurisdictional matters, the model narrows the definition of 'investment' and 'investor', and incorporates a 'denial of benefits' clause. On substantive matters, the model aims at narrowing the situations in which an indirect expropriation can be found, includes a closed list of conducts not linked to customary international law, that amount to a breach of Fair and Equitable Treatment (FET), and excludes references to 'legitimate expectations'. It also excludes from the most-favoured-nation clause the possibility of importation of substantive standards from other investment agreements (Duggal et al. 2019).

The previous four examples show how states seek to steer the system by narrowing the interpretation powers of arbitral tribunals. Moreover, these BIT models, though they could serve as navigation maps to offer guidelines to civil servants and diplomats while negotiating IIAs, at the end of the day the final wording of an IIA will depend more upon geopolitical and lobbying factors than on the mere fact of the country having a 'progressive' BIT model.

The third set of changes that have responded to the criticisms and to the different proposals promoted by IIL stakeholders are the negotiation and ratification of multilateral and bilateral binding IIAs. The most relevant example in this category is the Comprehensive and Economic Trade Agreement (CETA) between Canada and the EU. This binding treaty has been hailed as a treaty that has included important changes directed to guaranteeing the regulatory activity of the states, to create greater certainty and foreseeability on arbitral awards and reducing conflicts of interest by creating a semi-permanent arbitration tribunal.

Specifically, chapter 8 of the treaty creates a semi-permanent Investment Tribunal to resolve the conflicts between investors and host states. It also creates an appellate body to review the decisions reached by the panel in the first instance. This tribunal, created under the CETA framework, is comprised of fifteen members elected by the CETA mixed committee out of which five must be Canadian nationals, five must be nationals from any EU country and the other five should come from other states. These arbitrators have a five-year term and may be re-elected for a second five-year term. During their term as a member of the tribunal, all fifteen members receive a fee simply by being on the list. However, when a dispute arises, a division of three arbitrators out of the list of fifteen constitutes a sub-division panel in charge of resolving the dispute. These arbitrators selected to resolve the dispute will receive an additional payment.

The CETA creates an appellate tribunal that is entitled to confirm, modify or revoke the award issued by the sub-panel. The creation of this appellate body is innovative and new in the sense that in neither *ad hoc* tribunals nor institutional tribunals does an appellate body exist. The closest institutional arrangements to an appellate body are the ICSID annulment committees. The CETA agreement also creates a special regime of conflict of interest for the arbitrators. These regimes aim at avoiding situations in which arbitrators act as advisers or as expert witnesses for any of the CETA parties in situations of investment disputes. The CETA has been hailed as a model to be followed by other treaties as it partially responds to some of the criticisms against the IIL system, and specifically against the ISDS. However, it is important to consider that the court continues to offer privileged standing to foreign investors, and there is no requirement to exhaust domestic legal resources. Also, the structure does not avoid the possible economic incentives that could influence arbitrator's decision by seeking future appointments.

Finally, the fourth set of changes that have responded to the criticisms and to the different proposals promoted by IIL stakeholders are reflected in interpretative changes recently adopted by arbitral tribunals that have taken into consideration in their respective analyses other subsystems of International Law such as International Human Rights Law and International Environmental Law. The most notable case is *Philip Morris v Uruguay* in which the tribunal considered that the measures adopted by the government to reduce smoking in the country were pursued within its legitimate police powers (Philip Morris Brands Sàrl, Philip Morris Products S.A. and Abal Hermanos S.A. v. Oriental Republic of Uruguay (formerly, *FTR Holding SA, Philip Morris Products S.A. and Abal Hermanos S.A. v. Oriental Republic of Uruguay*) 2016). In this case, the tribunal used the margin of appreciation test, used mainly by the European Court of Human Rights, as understanding that states require certain spaces to develop their policies (Harten, Sovereign Choices and Sovereign Constrains 2013). A proportionality review was used by the investment tribunal and follows a three-stage test: (i) was the state measure suitable for a legitimate purpose of the state? (ii) was a less restrictive, but equally effective and reasonably feasible, measure available? (iii) does the measure balance cons and benefits appropriately? (Harten, Sovereign Choices and Sovereign Constrains 2013, 35). This mechanism that has also been used in the context of EU Law and the World Trade Organization (WTO) Law allows adjudicators to balance individual rights v collective interests (Harten, Sovereign Choices and Sovereign Constrains 2013).

AN AUTOPOIETIC SYSTEM

The term 'autopoiesis' or 'self-production' is a theory originally coined by the Chilean biologists Humberto Maturana and Francisco Varela in 1974 to describe the ability of living systems to self-reproduce. According to this theory, living systems are self-producing units that maintain their essential form, perpetuating themselves according to their internal organisation, while separating themselves from the environment (D'Amato 2014). The opposite to autopoiesis is allopoietic or 'other-produced' systems that, in contrast to autopoietic systems, are characterised by either having fixed elements that are unchangeable or that the elements of the system are produced by forces and factors in the environment (Jacobson 1989, 1660). As described by Jacobson:

> 'The core image of autopoiesis is the individual organism, ceaselessly generating elements out of elements, forming each element into an indissoluble unity from a more complex base of energy and matter' (Jacobson 1989). 'Elements that do not join the circular dance of autopoiesis are outside the system, part of its environment. They may affect elements in the system or be affected by them, but play no role in the operations reproducing the system'. (Jacobson 1989)

An autopoietic system is characterised by making internal operational changes responding to the external environment (outside pressure) in a controlled manner while always guaranteeing that the system itself is not dismantled. Internally controlled changes maintain the identity of the system regardless of whether or not the elements are the same. In other words, the system could be partially open to outside pressure, but the system responds to such pressure on its own terms (Jacobson 1989, 1661). An autopoietic system reproduces its elements by the interactions of its elements. The system also chooses the topics that are addressed by the system. Furthermore, the system has a clear structure that allows it to maintain its existence and identity. Moreover, the unity of the structure is possible through expectations as to how communications ought to develop past events linked with the future (Deggau 1988).

Although, the origin of the theory occurred in the field of biology, describing cells and organisms, this term has also been used to describe the operation of social systems. In this context, Niklas Luhman used the term to describe interactions of such social systems, as the law. In an autopoietic legal system, 'every "legal communication" must respond to a prior legal communication, and every legal communication must command a subsequent legal communication' (Jacobson 1989, 1665). An autopoietic legal system communicates within itself and also in a controlled manner with the external environment (Teubner 1988, 3).

In the context of this book, I am using the term to describe the IIL responses to criticism and challenges as described in the previous sections of this chapter. Autopoiesis is used as an analytical tool to understand the internal dynamics and interactions of the IIL system with the external world (the environment). The environment refers to outside institutions and non-initiated individuals (as described in chapter 4 of this book), that interact with the system. IIL is a self-motivated system and has been a system that resists outside forces. The ways in which IIAs are negotiated and by which arbitral tribunals assess each case, demonstrate that the IIL system is self-preserving and self-sustaining in the sense that it neither requires domestic law, nor other branches of PIL to justify its existence and operation. IIL and all its norms are valid just for the sake of existence. Its validity does not depend on extralegal forms that are not linked to it. IIL becomes self-referential, producing its own elements (Rosenfeld 1991).

The essential element for the reproduction of IIL is its internal network of communications that produce and reproduce communications, while creating identities and differences (Rosenfeld 1991). This allows the system 'to remain operationally severed both from extralegal norms and from the imprint of arbitrary subjectivity by relying on self-referential circularity as the foundation of law' (Rosenfeld 1991). The IIL system is also an autopoietic system in the sense that it defines its own openings and its closures. Of course, the concept of closure does not necessarily mean isolation (Luhman, Closure and Openness: On Reality in the World of Law 1988, 336). As stated by Luhman:

> The concept of autopoietic closure therefore initially states only that the recursive application of its own operation to the results of its own operations is an indispensable aspect of the system's reproduction. This defines the unity and autonomy of the system. (Luhman, Closure and Openness: On Reality in the World of Law 1988, 336).

IIL is in a constant dialectic relationship of being open and closed, normatively closed but cognitively open. The system is open to the environment, not in a sense that puts information into the system but in the sense of how the system responds to the pressures of the environment and how it interprets it. On the other hand, the closure of the system does not mean the absence of an environment. A closed system means that all operations always reproduce the system (Luhman, The Unity of the Legal System 1988).

A system is closed in the sense that it is the system that grants the quality of being accepted by IIL, and of its elements. 'The system therefore reproduces its elements by its elements by transferring this quality of meaning from moment to moment and thereby always providing new elements with normative validity. In this respect it is closed to the environment' (Luhman, The Unity of the Legal System 1988, 20). Cognitively open means its ability to determine whether the conditions have been met or not through the analysis of facts (Luhman, The Unity of the Legal System 1988). Hence, the facts can force the system to change its programmes if necessary, based on the facts. Furthermore, it is this ability that allows the system to maintain a relation with its environment.

In this context, and as analysed in the previous sections, IIL is a system that is under pressure to change and is taking an autopoietic response for such purposes. All the examples of initiatives described in the previous section, are mere variations, but do not amount to drastic or essential changes in the IIL system. In this sense, the action of self-preservation of the system has promoted discussions on mild reforms to ISDS, the development of Model BIT's and encouraging arbitral tribunals to be open to considering other branches of International Law such as International Human Rights Law.

The external factors are contributing to modulating internal normative formulations and to improving the system in the eyes of initiated and some non-initiated. In other words, the constant criticism against IIL and ISDS is compelling it to adapt in order to survive. The variations are determined by the system itself; for instance, the use of other regimes such as International

Human Rights Law is completely determined by the system itself. In generating self-controlled variations, IIL guarantees its survival and self-perpetuation while maintaining its essence and developing its own means of survival (D'Aspremont 2014). Its capacity to generate and control crisis, contradictions and destruction guarantees its self-regeneration as well as its capacity to maintain its own boundaries yet creating a clear separation from the environment (D'Aspremont 2014; Gilgen 2013).

It is also important to take into consideration that stakeholders within IIL have an interest in preserving it as they have invested time and energy in the system. Furthermore, in the case of arbitrators and attorneys, there is the implication of financial gain. As a result, any interpretation or action that is perceived as anti-homeostatic is automatically discarded and ruled out. Furthermore, IIL being an autopoietic system has sufficient autonomy to decide for itself what form of the environment it will use as its input and the output that reaches out to the environment (Luhman 2013, 30).

Nonetheless, it is important to find alternatives, and cut-short the dominant belief that the existing system can reproduce itself indefinitely through autopoiesis, and to explore alternatives to radically change it from the outside (the environment) and not from the inside (the system) as has happened. As stated by Lewis Gordon:

> *Disciplinary decadence is* the ontologizing or reification of a discipline. In such an attitude, we treat our discipline as thought as it was never born and has always existed and will never change or, in some cases, die. More than immortal, it is eternal. Yet as something that came into being, it lives, in such an attitude, as a monstrosity, as an instance of a human creation that can never die. Such perspective brings with it a special fallacy. Its assertion as absolute eventually leads to no room for other disciplinary perspectives, the result of which is the rejection of them for not being one´s own. Thus, if one's discipline has foreclosed the question of its scope, all that is left is a form of applied work. Such work militates against thinking. (L. Gordon 2015)

This reflection should lead insiders to reflect on the functioning of the system and how the system re-enacts itself to guarantee its existence. It is important for insiders to be open for alternative ways of thinking that may include changing the understanding of the system as we know it. As highlighted by Amical Cabral, economic and cultural resistances are essential for developing countries to survive in this wild capitalism (Cabral 2016, 78).

CONCLUSION

As has been described in this chapter, IIL is an autopoietic system in the sense that it has its own internal communication networks, it is self-motivated, self-preserving, and self-sustaining in the sense that it neither requires domestic law, nor other branches of Public International Law to justify its existence and operation. Nonetheless, the IIL system and the ISDS as its main mechanism of enforcing IIA obligations have been subject to criticisms.

The criticisms surrounding IIL and specifically the ISDS arise out of the fact that the system is non-coherent, encrypted, responds to a neoliberal ideology, and makes it difficult for the host state to foresee whether a certain sovereign regulatory decision could breach an obligation contained in an IIA. In this context, the IIL and specifically the ISDS are responding to the criticisms by adopting controlled strategies. These controlled strategies send messages to the environment of being open to the outside without directly making substantive changes that could jeopardise the essence of the IIL system, namely the offer of enhanced protection to foreign investors, and giving priority to the market over other structural elements such as the obligation of a state to promote and to protect human rights.

Accordingly, and as described in this chapter, the IIL system and ISDS have adopted four sets of strategies to move forward making certain but not substantive changes. These four strategies are as follows: (i) the procedural reform discussions of ICSID and UNCITRAL; (ii) the development of Model BITs that narrow the scope and clarify certain IIA terms; (iii) negotiation and ratification of binding multilateral and bilateral binding IIA that include progressive clauses such as the creation of a quasi-permanent tribunal; (iv) arbitral tribunals broadening their analyses incorporating arguments from other branches of International Law such as International Human Rights Law. As described in this chapter; such strategies do not mean deep changes in either the logic or the operation of the system.

Considering that IIL is an autopoietic system and that its responses to the pressure coming from the outside environment for it to change and re-adapt are also autopoietic, the strategies described herein must be taken with a pinch of salt in the sense that the system and all its downfalls, as described in the previous chapters of this book, will continue to be part of the system. The challenge is to move away from the IIL system and the ISDS either by bringing it down or by making profound and meaningful changes to the system, dismantling its autopoietic way of functioning and responding to the interests of stake holders but more importantly to communities and the collective good.

Conclusion

IIL AS AN INSTRUMENT OF SYSTEMIC VIOLENCE

As I have described in the previous chapters, the International Investment Law (IIL) system is presented as beneficial for all the stake holders in what is portrayed as a win-win-win situation for everyone (states, Multinational Corporations -MNCs, society). Its supporters argue that the IIL system is technocratic, objective, depoliticised (particularly as it has become an alternative to gunboat diplomacy and direct diplomatic protection) and an appropriate instrument for the attraction of Foreign Direct Investment (FDI) to peripheral countries that is said to be essential for their economic development. Furthermore, it is also argued that countries enter into International Investment Agreements (IIAs) on a voluntary basis, having had the opportunity as sovereign states to negotiate the terms of the treaty.

However, as set out in this book, the reality surrounding the IIL system ranges beyond the arguments that defend the benefits of the system. Contemporary IIL appeared in the international arena as a response to the decolonisation processes that took place during the second half of the twentieth century. IIL became an instrument to maintain certain levels of legal, political and economic control upon former colonies and other territories that previously were under imperial rule.

The neoliberal ideological shift of 1970s, ignited by the economic conditions of the time, also played in favour of strengthening the IIL system world-wide. Developing countries shifted their priorities from defending their sovereign rights and independently managing their internal affairs, to join the global market. They sought to create a political and legal environment that was suitable to attract the foreign investment, which was considered essential if they were to reach their promised land of development.

Developing countries joined the IIL system expecting to attract the benefits promised by FDI, following the equation: IIA = FDI = Development. However, countries were not necessarily aware of the real scope of the terms of the treaty to which they were agreeing, thereby surrendering up their ability to regulate on issues of public interest such as the environment, health or basic facilities, among others.

Another important aspect to highlight is that the negotiation capacity of developing countries is to an extent limited in the sense that the thirst for FDI leads them to accept the terms imposed by developed countries in IIAs. Indeed, the negotiation between capital exporters and Third World countries does not occur within a context of reciprocity. This is as a result of these states' socio-economic limitations (the direct consequence of the colonial and imperial projects) and their geopolitical position on the world stage. This situation translates into developing countries having limited spaces to discuss or to make significant changes or amendments to the terms of the treaties. In fact, as it has been pointed out several times, it is no coincidence that the majority of IIAs, worldwide, have the same patterns and structure. In reality, IIAs are the fallout from an economic battle where the strongest state secures the best investment and trade treaties for its industries.

The acceptance of the terms of the treaties happens within the context of a developmentalism discourse, a neoliberal ideology, an encrypted language and an autopoietic response. This, therefore, constructs a framework whereby Third World countries are supposed to be satisfied with relying upon the exploitation of their natural resources by foreign investors (as they have the technology to do so) while offering cheap, indebted labour as the means of surviving in the capitalist system.

The IIL system is structured to protect the economic interests of foreign investors and to offer to that investor solutions to any problem or risk that could arise with the host state. In doing so, the system allows foreign investors to challenge any act *jure imperii* adopted by any public authority of the host state whenever such foreign investors consider that their economic interests have been affected. The possibility of challenging decisions adopted by public authorities of the host country before an international arbitral tribunal translates into placing individuals, corporations and states on a notionally equal footing. As a consequence, a company that represents millions of dollars is entitled to challenge measures adopted by any state authority that is acting on behalf of millions of people.

In protecting the economic interests of foreign investors, the IIL system acts as a deterrent against actions by host state public authorities as it could impact the public decision-making process. States may be reticent to act in order to avoid being forced into international litigation and to potentially be found liable to pay exaggerated sums of money as compensation. That ability to challenge regulations in any of its forms (law, internal judicial decisions, decrees, among others) threatens the ability of governments, especially those of states in which social conditions are problematic, to regulate and to protect the enjoyment of rights.

To paraphrase Michael Foucault, the interest of the market and of its main players (foreign investors) became one of the main reasons to confront governments and their laws (Foucault 2008). It is also important to point to the fact that IIAs only create obligations on the host state and not on the foreign investor. This clearly results in an imbalanced system that grants *locus standing* to MNCs to directly challenge states. In this regard, such protective treaties place foreign investors above the *polis* by protecting only the rights of investors above essential interests of the host country.

The IIL system is structured to satisfy the interests of foreign investors and to secure the correct functioning of the market, regardless of issues of human rights, the environment and labour standards, among other relevant aspects (M. Sornarajah 2017). At the same time, the system that has been shaped and influenced by neoliberal ideology, also reproduces such patterns and serves as a vehicle for spreading neoliberalism, hailing more individuals while implementing neoliberal-based policies world-wide (M. Sornarajah 2017).

Domestic regulations and judicial operators in peripheral countries are presented as not robust enough to guarantee investor rights. The local courts are similarly considered to be not good enough to resolve a dispute that could exist between an investor and the host state for many alleged reasons including a of lack of neutrality, lack of expertise vis-à-vis the specific forward-looking vision, a lack of understanding of the language allegedly required to deal with investment and financial affairs, and the lack of time. This distrust of peripheral judicial systems justified the consolidation of this legal framework for risk-management that at best hedges MNCs economic interests against and over all others and at worst contributes to blurring the line between security and economic development interests and concerns. In this regard, in 1901 Elihu Root stated the following:

> The simplest form of protection is that exercised by strong countries whose citizens are found in parts of the earth under the jurisdiction of governments whose control is inadequate for the preservation of order. Under such circumstances in times of special disturbance it is an international custom for the countries having the power to intervene directly for the protection of their own citizens, as in the case of the Boxer rebellion in China, when substantially all the Western powers were concerned in the march to Pekin and the forcible capture of that city for the protection of the legations. (Root 1910)

The IIL system and specifically its Investment State Dispute Settlement (ISDS) procedure has been hailed as an important advancement in the protection of foreign investors´ rights and in the peaceful settlement of disputes. It is argued that ISDS offers the benefit that conflicts are resolved by individuals with relevant expertise and more expeditiously than in domestic courts. It is argued that investment arbitrations depoliticise the claim, thereby making it more useful for the protection of the rights of foreign investors; it is also a shorter and swifter procedure.

Other arguments include that an arbitrator can be better qualified and have better skills and knowledge than domestic judges in peripheral countries. Arbitration is presented as the ideal option as it allows the existence of a neutral and independent forum whenever a conflict arises between the foreign investor and the host state (Greider 2001). The problem arises because arbitral tribunals assess the legality of acts *jure imperii*, be they in the form of a law, an administrative act or a judicial decision, not from the perspective of the common good or based upon he terms of a domestic Constitution (as a representation of the people's voice), or for contextual reasons, such as the protection of the environment or the response to the Covid-19 catastrophe, but based upon clauses of the relevant IIA's and, beyond that, on an economic neoliberal logic (Lang 2011).

Scratching below the surface of the technocratic objectivity and political neutrality of the IIL system one finds epistemic violence. This violence is represented in the form of a monopoly over 'expert' language and the colonial/racial use of time as a principle for classifying North/South societies. As held out, the egalitarianism of arbitration is 'notional' (as opposed to 'real') insofar as it violently imposes the obligation to 'pay to regulate' on supposedly sovereign governments thereby stripping them of their (right to) self-determination, that is, 'colonialism by other means'.

The power granted to investment arbitrators is partially derived from the fact that IIL discourse is 'encrypted' in the sense of being a construction of a mysterious specific code-discourse founded upon vagueness and technicality to prevent the non-initiated (outsiders) from having unauthorised access and use of the IIL discourse, thereby creating extra-layers. In doing so, the IIL discourse asserts a monopoly over a certain language that expresses and positivises the forward-looking vision and imagination.

This paradoxical formation that asserts universality, only to turn around and deny it to some, creates, on the one hand, a class who as set out in this book must be conceived as the 'initiated' who are entitled to decrypt the encrypted discourse. On the other hand, though, it hides from view the actual relationships and exercising of power. This actually pre-empts popular formations from gaining access to the power-knowledge space that rules over global financial investment relations or frustrates their efforts to do so. This creates areas of socio-political exclusion and facilitates situations of social and political control. As presented in this work, the encryption of the IIL discourse is linked to the unchallenged acceptance of Western epistemological superiority as well as to forms of power. This epistemological superiority as well as the forms of power are a phenomenon rooted in colonial relationships persisting after the processes of decolonisation.

The encryption of IIL discourse grants power to the initiated sitting in investment arbitral tribunals who can adjudicate over the exceptional time and space of global investment relations, reach decisions, impose huge sums of money as compensation upon host states, and thereby have a direct impact on domestic policy and on the behaviour of the host country as well as on the human rights claims of its peoples. Moreover, as the encryption creates insiders and outsiders (legitimated and non-legitimated to speak the IIL's discourse), it limits political participation and accountability of the host states and its authorities. The existence of an international system for the protection of foreign assets, as an alternative to domestic courts, resembles the colonial past when foreigners from Western colonial powers benefitted from special legal treatment in the colonies as well as in other independent countries subjugated by the West.

Under the surface mask of technocratic objectivity, political neutrality and appropriateness, Western countries 'were able to impose on developing countries their view of a liberal and protective international framework, which the customary process failed to achieve.' (Wouters, Sanderijn and Hachez 2013, 25). Hence, the normative monopoly allowed Western legal concepts and principles to be imposed initially through FCN, and later through IIAs upon peripheral countries, thereby legitimising repressive and plundering actions of capital-exporting states.

Due to many criticisms, the IIL as an autopoietic system is undergoing discussions to pursue changes. Some investment arbitral tribunals are becoming more open to considering police power arguments for the protection of human rights, the environment and health. However, and as explained in this book, the discussions and the ongoing changes do not signify deep changes to the system. Rather, they are mild responses to protect the long-term existence of the system. To sum up, and as presented in previous chapters of this book, the IIL system allows foreign investors to roll out all the international legal infrastructure against host states to protect their economic interests, just as when the colonial powers 'were quick to roll out the cannon to protect their investment' (Piketty 2014, 458). Hence, it is possible to say that in the twentieth century, the bayonets have become international treaties which follow the same aim of protecting the economic interest of the West and its companies.

FROM COLONIALISM TO THE AGE OF DEVELOPMENT

The alternative narrative that I have presented in this work has focused on how the International Investment Law (IIL) system facilitates systemic violence. The alternative narrative advances a contention that may seem modestly original and yet crucially important: we get to capitalism in the twenty-first century if and only if we posit the question concerning the ways in which the state and society, regulation as well as production, can be financed. If the answer is 'through (private) direct or indirect investment', then the importance of the IIL system becomes apparent and cannot be overstated.

IIL is presented as a system of rules to protect investors from uncertainty and risk, which ends up becoming a system of norms establishing the 'normal' conduct of states limiting their capacity to self-regulation. Put simply and perhaps even bluntly, the establishment of IIL asserts the primacy of (capitalist) values over the lives of entire nations and peoples. It 'democratises' and 'globalises' capital in a perverse way, and then shields such perversion, making its unjust core non-apparent.

This protection goes on creating a global legal framework that facilitates accumulation of profit and the movement of investors and capital worldwide while, at the same time, reducing costs and all the while securing and maintaining privileged access to natural resources under an investor-friendly international legal system.

As emphasised in this work part of the dynamic, from colonial times forward, was for capitalist entrepreneurs from central economies to seek economic opportunities abroad, particularly in the periphery, that could allow them to obtain major economic returns and thereby increase the levels of accumulation. After the decolonisation processes of the second half of the twentieth century, the Manichean division between 'civilised' and 'savage' (coloniser and colonised) was rewritten in accordance with the new reality of world politics, rebranding the distinction in terms of developed and underdeveloped nations (Escobar 1995, 80). This approach was strengthened by an evolutionist Eurocentric perspective that perceived development as a unilineal process in which Europe was ahead leading the social evolution path (Quijano 2000, 311). In this context, the world was 'divided between Euro-American developers and "irresponsible" developees living in a late twentieth-century version of the state of nature: the wretched and infinitely poor (Guardiola-Rivera, Story of a Death Foretold: The Coup Against Salvador Allende, 11 September 1973 2013, 126). The concept of development has different meanings for different people and can even have different uses (Baxi 2009). The two main narratives that include the different perspectives of development can be summarised on the one hand: in the narrative of development, as developmentalism discourse, as presented in this work, and development as hope.

Developmentalism discourse focuses on highlighting a linear time process of evolution of societies that turn a blind eye to past colonialism and imperialism and, rather, focuses on showing a complete process achieved by Euro-American societies. It follows that this focuses on the functioning of the market, wealth maximisation and economic growth (Baxi 2009). Breton Woods' institutions, specifically the International Monetary Fund (IMF) and the World Bank (WB), played a key role in the fast embracement of the IIL system and neoliberal ideology around the world (Prieto-Rios 2015). The private sector, specifically private foreign investment, was considered very important and relevant in contributing to the path of development in Third World countries. By way of example, the 1992 World Bank's Guidelines on the Treatment of Foreign Direct Investment reflect this position (The World Bank Group 1992). FDI was portrayed as essential for development and modernisation of Third World countries, especially considering the technological dependence so as to exploit natural resources, to produce manufactured goods and to improve local infrastructure. In this form, the IMF and the WB played an important role in pursuing the embrace of neoliberal ideology and the developmental discourse among Third World countries (both essential for the promotion of the IIL system world-wide).

The alternative is the narrative of development as a space of hope in the struggle, whereby development can have some counter-hegemonic possibilities, seeking the redistribution of rights, agency, capabilities, among other things and seeking progress. This approach is currently centred on the discussion of the right to development (Baxi 2009). Considering that topic of research, the narrative used in this chapter and in the book in general is on the developmentalism discourse. As part of the developmentalism discourse, to be a developing country is portrayed as the result of failures of individuals and societies rather than the result of a systemic or structural violence which has a long history and roots in the colonial past (Coronil 2000). Hence, developing countries are required to adapt and to make the necessary changes to reach the goal of development. The aspirational dream of becoming developed facilitated a race to the bottom among developing countries to attract foreign investment, specifically FDI. Developing countries raced to attract FDI as an essential part of their economic growth and development (among other things). This competition simultaneously deepened the divisions among developing countries, and resembled the old colonial practice of dividing colonised continents for the benefit of the colonisers. Nonetheless, and as presented in this book, the relationship between FDI and a clear path to reach the aspiration of development is not unanimous.

Development became the perfect way to justify, and to legitimise, policies of control upon developing countries. It created, in the collective imagination, the idea that it is possible to change the status of a country from a peripheral to a central country. In this way, the developmentalism discourse has served as a pretext to justify (using Fanon's analysis) the occupation of every single aspect of the society and life of developing countries. Accordingly, the developmentalism discourse played a very important role in the consolidation of the IIL system world-wide. IIAs were presented as the most suitable instruments for the attraction of foreign investments, specifically FDI. Nonetheless, the IIL system, with its IIA, fulfills the aim of disciplining how states should behave towards foreign investments, just as an adult addresses a child, patronising her, telling her what to do.

In this process of consolidation of the IIL system, neoliberalism as an ideological project also played an important role. On the one hand, the operation of the system is marked by a distrust of government regulations and its activities while at the same time underpinning the idea that the market and its actors should operate without any type of unnecessary intervention by the state. In this context, IIL acts as a tool to limit regulatory activity and, as such, state intervention in the market and its involvement with market stakeholders. Nonetheless, the last sixty years of history have showed that the magic recipes of development have not functioned as expected. Thus, the dream of redemption by reaching development has become a 'history of the loss of illusions' (Escobar 1995, 4) where the promised land of development and abundance became unreachable. In this regard, it is important for developing countries, for international financial institutions, and society in general, to rethink the role of the IIL system.

THE NEW BENEFICIARIES OF THE SYSTEM

The global economy has experienced different changes since the end of the twentieth century and the complexity of the world economy challenges traditional classifications. One important change is the expansion of the Manichean division among countries, moving from a simple binary classification of developed and developing to a more plural sub-division in terms of income. The IMF classifies countries as advanced economies, emerging markets, and developing economies (Nielsen 2011; The World Bank n.d.). The World Bank, which has put itself upon a pedestal as the expert on global development, uses different charts and classifications, classifying developing countries into low, middle and upper-middle income countries.

Although to use IMF and World Bank classifications in a critical work may be counter-intuitive, the idea is to show how world financial institutions recognise economic changes experienced world-wide, and that economic periphery countries have also started to play the capitalist game by increasing macro-economic conditions. Peripheral countries have also become exporters of capital as in the case of Brazil that has been playing a significant role becoming a country with relevant investments not only in Latinamerica but in different countries in Africa. However, it can be also argued that this plural subdivision hides the continuing existing division between the holders of knowledge and wealth on the one hand and the 'others' in the North-South relationship.

It is important to acknowledge that in the new global economic and political reality, 'Nation States, as units in a complex interactive system, are not very likely to be the long term arbiters of the relationship between globality and modernity' (Appadurai 1996, 19). Nation-state ability to regulate internally, to benefit from the activities of its individuals and its companies in the global market is constantly challenged as a result of various factors, including economic factors such as the flow of capital, and also the international legal structure IIL (Appadurai 1996).

The romantic vision of the nation-state as the unit that adopts decisions as a sovereign and independent entity is no longer workable in the current condition of the global market. Nation-states are navigating uncharted waters where grassroots populations want to regain their rights to decide their own affairs, something which is impossible as result of the existing interstate international relations and international law. In this context, Arjun Appadurai argues that it is necessary for the populations and the individuals to think beyond the nation-state to construct apparatuses for a post-national social form (Appadurai 1996). Appaudari's arguments written in 1996 may seem to fall short considering the current world reality whereby nationalism and isolation seem to be ruling the economic world in the heads of politicians of the sort of Trump in the USA or Boris Johnson in the United Kingdom.

Despite of the foregoing, and without pursuing a deep analysis and a systematic critique of the situations of countries whereby politicians seems to be promoting isolation, a quick glance at the current global market realities shows that MNCs continue to exercise an important role in influencing political decisions. It is also important to highlight that isolation will not stop MNCs continuing to operate on a global scale as the international legal structure allows MNCs to be incorporated in any country of the world directly or indirectly through subsidiaries.

A brief check of the polices adopted by the forty-fifth President of the USA during the first weeks of his Administration, shows that the role and the independence of the state from global corporate interests is not that evident. For instance, Mr Trump's election pledge promoted the reduction of unnecessary regulations on companies' activities (Trump 2020). Furthermore, the policies defended by the former USA president benefited industries such as pharmaceuticals, oil, gas, coal and defence (Monica 2017). It is also important to highlight that Trump's cabinet had a strong ties with MNCs. For instance, Trump's Vice-president Mike Pence has ties to Koch Industries, and Rex Tillerson has ties with Exxon Mobile (Weissman 2017). There is no much difference with President Joe Biden who has links with Wall Street and Silicon Valley (Harnik 2020).

The Trump administration re-negotiated some treaties including NAFTA in order to obtained greater economic benefits. Hence, on the one hand, the Trump administration acted according to the logic of capitalism, in the sense of negotiating treaties to obtained better economic benefits for the strong countries; on the other hand, it did not bother renegotiating treaties with peripheral Third World Countries that are not relevant or important in the global market competitive race.

With the broad analysis of some of the economic policies put forward by the former US president Donald Trump, it is possible to perceive that, in economic terms, no very important change will happen under president Joe Biden´s administration, in the sense of the relationship between governments and MNCS. Hence, the porous nature of the nation state vis à vis MNCs interests continues being relevant in the current global economic order, even under the circumstances whereby nation states seek to regain their roles as protagonists.

The United States, the United Kingdom and other central states that throughout history have economically benefited from their central positions are not necessarily in a condition of being the puppeteers of the economic world. Nowadays, Western countries play a limited role in a globalised economic system. The capitalist system is becoming an entity on its own, where capital moves around the globe according to its needs, and where MNCs are benefiting from the economic and legal framework created for the system to work.

The negotiation of IIAs happens within a corporate atmosphere whereby proxies of MNCs actively participate in such discussions (Miles 2013). Thus, transforming into a type of commercial diplomacy in which the private sector has further involvement in bilateral relations between countries. The foregoing is evident not only due to the fact that corporations and MNCs participate in bilateral and multilateral treaty negotiations but also due to the fact that overseas diplomatic missions have business representatives, who consistently join activities pursued by Ministries of Foreign Affairs and Trade Ministers.

A very relevant example of the involvement of corporations and MNCs in negotiations of international trade and investment treaties occurred in the case of the Free Trade Area of the Americas (FTAA). When the negotiations of the FTAA were about to kick off, twenty-nine U.S. multinationals signed a letter requesting that the treaty should have the same investor provision as the NAFTA (Greider 2001). Another example happened when U.S. based multinational corporations under the auspices of the U.S. Intellectual Property Committee procured the inclusion of intellectual property as a trade issue within the Uruguay Round and later in the conclusion of the World Trade Organisation (WTO) Agreement on Trade Related Aspects of Intellectual Property Rights (TRIPS) (Miles, The Origins of International Investment Law: Empire, Environment and The Safeguard of Capital 2013).

In the specific case of the IIL system, corporations have actively participated in pursuing the execution of more treaties among countries to widen the global network of treaties, and thereby strengthening the entire system. This results in their enjoying a global supranational protection of their assets and their economic benefits. In this regard, Kate Miles expresses the following:

> The origins of foreign investment protection entwined government with private commercial interests. More recent alignment of state and investor interests has manifested in a variety of ways. The escalation in state activity in securing bilateral investment treaties has been attributed to the push of foreign investors for more secure and predictable legal regimes to protect investment. (Miles, International Investment Law: Origins, Imperialism and Conceptualizing the Environment 2010)

MNCs are legally structured to limit shareholder liability and to operate in different jurisdictions in order to maximise profits while also enjoying global protection via BITs and FTAs (see the case of *Philip Morris v. Australia*). The foregoing is troubling considering the reality that we are experiencing a corporate globalisation (Coronil 2000), where corporations control the world economy. Corporations are holders of improved-everyday technology, that allows them to transform natural resources into goods and to capture new biological elements to offer in the market (Coronil 2000).

MNCs have become a contradiction by becoming, in certain instances stateless entities, despite being incorporated in many states through corporate structures such as subsidiaries. Furthermore, MNCs are made up of known and anonymous shareholders, some natural persons and other legal entities such as pension funds. Nowadays, it is difficult to find one MNC that is majority-owned by one capitalist; the closest are MNCs where there is a dominant shareholder who has a controlling stake by owning more than

20 per cent (Piketty 2014). MNCs owned by several shareholders can be of two types: preferred shareholders who have priority at dividend distribution but do not have votes on key decisions, and ordinary shareholders who have the right to vote.

Finally, and before concluding, I will briefly touch upon the natural persons that are behind MNCs, and who enjoy the economic benefits. The claim is that subjects who benefit economically from the activity of MNCs in their position as shareholders belong to a select group of individuals who form part of a global capitalist elite that benefit from global markets where beneficiaries are diffuse and where there is a huge inequality among individuals in the world (Piketty 2014). In order to shed some light on this argument, it is relevant to bring certain figures to the discussion. For instance, 4.5 million individuals, out of 4.5 billion possess on average a fortune of 10 million Euros the equivalent of 200 times the average global wealth of 60.000 Euros per individual. Furthermore, '[t]he top thousandth seem to own nearly 20 percent of total global wealth today, the top centile about 50 percent, and the top decile somewhere between 80 and 90 percent'. (Piketty 2014, 438).

Capitalism is keen on increasing the level of wealth of certain portions of society which are deemed to be the economically fittest. Of course, in this development, original advantages are not taken into consideration. It is expected that the benefit to a few will bring benefits to society in general (trickle-down economics) which has become the 'state of affairs since the late twentieth century' (Guardiola-Rivera 2010, 55). Although capitalists from developed industrialised countries, imposed themselves upon capitalists from less-developed countries, it is also true that wealthy class capitalists from emerging countries are becoming part of the global elite capitalists (Forbes 2013).

The existence of a global class of capitalists with more wealth than the average person allows the existence of groups of people able to have political, economic and cultural power domestically and also internationally by being able to stir the global structure for their own economic benefit. As power holders, capitalists can use their power for their own benefit, protecting and increasing their capital (Dussel 2014). The foregoing materialises in capitalists being able to use the geopolitical power and the bureaucracy of central states to protect and enhance their economic power and interests world-wide, while at the same time using non-developed countries to maintain friendly policies towards foreign capital. This class of global capitalists counts upon their power to defend their interests. In the past, it was military supported; nowadays, it is militarily and juridically supported. Hence, it is evident how MNCs are no longer working for the benefit of their home country, but rather for the economic benefit of the MNCs themselves, and shareholders as well the global capitalists behind the corporative structure.

OUTPUT AND FURTHER WORK

As mentioned at the beginning of this book, this work is the result of my pressing need to contest and challenge the IIL system from my standpoint as a Third World Academic, analysing and creating awareness about the imbalances of the system and the facilitation of situations of systemic violence. In this context, the argument that I have presented was that the IIL system is an instrument that facilitates systemic violence thanks to its network of treaties and arbitral tribunals as well as the vectors of encryption, its neoliberal ideology and its autopoietic process to face changes and criticisms.

I have pursued an inquiry problematising the production of 'truths' in the IIL system. In doing so, I have adopted an interdisciplinary approach bringing together a historical materialism, political, economic and legal analysis challenging some of the existing knowledge and common assumptions related to the IIL system. In pursuing this problematisation, this work has shown how the IIL system allowed multinational corporations (MNCs) to exercise control over Third World countries in order to protect their economic interests, and more specifically their ability to accumulate and increase profits.

The book has also shown that in giving priority to the market and its most important players, MNCs, the IIL system has become an instrument that facilitates situations of systemic violence that have a direct effect on individuals in Third World countries, especially the most vulnerable parts of those societies. In this sense, there is a need to rethink IIL, changing it from an instrument that facilitates international systemic violence to an instrument of positive change. For it to attain this objective, it will require re-building the whole structure from zero – but thinking about possible ways to change the whole structure, will form a part of a different work.

Moreover, it is important to bear in mind that Fanon highlighted the importance of the Third World starting over with a 'new Man' and that it is this aspect that it is necessary that the Third World, not continue along the path of subjugation but to be stronger parties in global relations (Fanon 2004). Accordingly, a relevant aspect that will require further research in the context of re-building the whole IIL system is to explore further ethical theories of groundlessness, radical investment and the heteronomy of law of the kind advanced by the late Ernesto Laclau, or by Lewis R. Gordon. Additionally, it is important to treat post-colonial claims as a constructive trust that accrues value over time and to undertake further work related to the right to development.

As mentioned in the introduction, this work does not offer a blueprint or a list of solutions. Rather, it expects readers to end up with more questions than solutions and with innovative ideas to pursue further research that could contribute to discovering ways to resist the global process experienced under the IIL system. Despite not being a blueprint, the author suggests some possible tracks and threads of future enquiry as follows.

Some relevant challenges lay ahead regarding the IIL system, some of those include how to make local government accountable over decisions that are reached in a global arena but which have a direct repercussion on citizens and communities of a determined country. It is also important to reflect on the fact that here is a global need for the redistribution of wealth and technology and that international investment law could be the catapult for such a change.

Another line of inquiry may focus on whether arbitrators and government officials are aware that some negative effects could exist by reason of how treaties are written and/or the decisions adopted by tribunals. Specifically, as to whether there is full knowledge that the treaty terms or an arbitral award may cause or contribute to the existence of situations of plunder, exploitation and the maintenance of situations of socio-economic asymmetric relationships.

Perhaps, considering alternatives to the orthodox policies of FDI (as other countries have dared to do) may break the vicious circle of economic dependence and dependence upon foreign investment that has characterised the Third World since colonial times. The foregoing is posited as economic dependence and the limitations experienced by capital-importer countries resemble colonial and imperial practices. It is clear that dependence upon foreign investment grants a leverage of control to investor capitalists, to capital exporter countries and to international financial agencies over Third World countries.

Another challenge is the need to rethink the role of markets in society, whether this should be given to markets and MNCs, and whether all goods should be allowed to be profitable or whether another approach should be taken. As an example, the priority given to the market and the rights of MNCs has caused ongoing challenges and struggles between communities and MNCs in the Third World, especially in the extraction of resources.

Finally, I consider that this construction can be used as a theoretical framework for a critical interdisciplinary analysis of other branches of International Economic Law – IEL. The foregoing is based upon the understanding that any form of IEL works within the framework of a neoliberal capitalist system which has been affected by a colonial past, that relies upon a specific form of discourse, and which is likely to produce situations of systemic violence within Third World countries.

Bibliography

Agosin, Manuel R. 2010. "Is Foreign Investment Always Good for Development?" In *Rethinking Foreign Investment for Sustainable Development: Lessons for Latin America*, edited by Kevin P. Gallagher and Daniel Chudnovsky. London: Anthem Press.

Agosin, Manuel R., and Ricardo Mayer. 1993. *Agreement Between the UK and Argentina for the Promotion and Protection of Investments*. July 28. Accessed June 28, 2020. https://www.gov.uk/government/publications/agreement-between-the-uk-and-argentina-for-the-promotion-and-protection-of-investments.

———. 2000. "Foreign Investment in Developing Countries: Does It Crowd in Domestic Investment?" *UNCTAD Discussion Papers*. February N/A. Accessed April 2020. http://unctad.org/en/Docs/dp_146.en.pdf.

Althusser, Louis. 1964. *Part Seven. Marxism and Humanism*. Accessed September 25, 2020. https://www.marxists.org/reference/archive/althusser/1964/marxism-humanism.htm.

———. 1971. *Lenin and Philosophy and Other Essays*. Translated by Ben Brewster. New York: Monthly Review Press.

———. 2014. *On the Reproduction of Capitalism: Ideology and Ideological State Apparatuses*. Translated by G. M. Goshgarian. London: Verso.

Anderson, Mark. 2014. *Aid to Africa: Donations from West Mask '$60bn Looting' of Continent*. July 15. Accessed June 4, 2020. https://www.theguardian.com/global-development/2014/jul/15/aid-africa-west-looting-continent.

Andon, Sergio Pita. 2019. «V.I.T.R.I.O.L.» *Iluminando*. 25 de Marzo. Último acceso: 14 de 1 de 2021. http://iluminando.org/2019/03/25/v-i-t-r-i-o-l/.

Anghie, Antony. 2007. *Imperialism, Sovereignty and the Making of International Law*. Cambridge: Cambridge University Press.

Appadurai, Arjun. 1996. *Modernity at Large: Cultural Dimensions of Globalization*. University of Minnesota Press.

———. 2016. *Banking on Words*. Chicago: The University of Chicago Press.

Arendt, Hannah. 1970. *On Violence*. New York, London: Harcourt, Brace & World, INC.
Atlas Economic Research Foundation. n.d. *Our History*. Accessed September 25, 2020. https://www.atlasnetwork.org/about/our-story.
Azurix Corp. v. The Argentine Republic. 2006. No. ARB/01/12 (ICSID Case).
Bacchus, James, and Jeffrey Sachs. 2020. "Why We Need a Moratorium on Investment Disputes During COVID-19." *ISDS*. June 9. Accessed November 6, 2020. https://isds.bilaterals.org/?why-we-need-a-moratorium-on.
Bakan, Joel. 2005. *The Corporation: The Pathological Pursuit of Profit and Power*. London: Constable & Robinson Ltd.
Barklem, Courtenay, and Enrique Prieto-Rios. 2011. "The Concept of "Indirect Expropiation", Its Appearance in the International System and Its Effect in the Regulatory Activity of Governments." *Civilizar* 11 (21): 77–98.
Baxi, Uprenda. 2009. *Human Rights in a Post-Human World: Critical Essays*. Oxford: University Oxford Press.
Becker, Colleen. 2013. "Aby Warburg's Pathosformel as Methodological Paradigm." *Journal of Art Historiography* 9: 1–25.
Benjamin, Walter. 1996. *Critique of Violence*. In *Walter Benjamin Selected Writings 1913–1926*, edited by Marcus Bullock and Michael W. Jennings, Vol. 1, 236–252. Cambirdge, MA: The Belknap Press of Harvard University Press.
———. 2007. *Illuminations*. Edited by Hannah Arendt. Translated by Harry Zohn. New York: Shocken Books.
Bernasconi-Osterwalder, N., and E. Brown Weiss. 2005. "International Investment Laws and Water: Learning from NAFTA Experience." In *Fresh Water and International Economic Law*, edited by E. Brown Weiss, L. Boisson de Chazournes, and N. Bernasconi-Osterwalder. Oxford: Oxford University Press.
Bernasconi-Osterwalder, Nathalie, and Rheea Tamara Hoffman. 2012. "The German Nuclear Phase-Out Put to the Test in International Investment Arbitration?: Background to the new dispute Vattenfall v Germany (II)." *International Institute for Sustainable Development*. Accessed Septemmber 25, 2020. https://www.iisd.org/system/files/publications/german_nuclear_phase_out.pdf.
Bernstein, Peter L. 1953. "Profit Theory: Where Do We Go from Here." *The Quarterly Journal of Economics* 67 (3): 407.
Birch, Kean, and Vlad Mykhnenko. 2010. "A World Turned Right Way Up." In *The Rise and Fall of Neoliberalism: The Collapse of an Economic Order?*, edited by Kean Birch and Vlad Mykhnenko. London: Zed Books.
Blundell, John. 2015. *Waging the War of Ideas*. London: The Institute of Economic Affairs.
Bottini, Gabriel. 2016. "Present and Future of ICSID Annulment: The Path to an Appellate Body?" *ICSID Review* 31 (3): 712–727.
Brown, Wendy. 2005. *Edgework: Critical Essays on Knowledge and Politics*. Princeton, NJ: Princeton University Press.
Bryant, Levi R. 2011. *The Democracy of Objects*. Ann Arbor: Open Humanities Press.
Bulhan, Hussain Abidlahi. 1985. *Frantz Fanon and the Psychology of Oppression*. New York and London: Plenum Press.

Butler, Eamonn. n.d. *A Short History of the Mont Pelerin Society: Based on a History of the Mont Pelerin Society by Max Hartwell.* Accessed September 25, 2020. https://www.montpelerin.org/wp-content/uploads/2015/12/Short-History-of-MPS-2014.pdf.

Cabral, Amical. 2016. *Resistance and Decolonization.* Translated by Dan Wood. London and New York: Rowman & Littlefield.

Caplin, Andrew, and Kala Krishna. 1998. "Tariffs and the Most Favoured Nation Clause: A Game Theoretic-Approach." *Seoul Journal of Economics* 1 (3): 267.

Carlston, Kenneth S. 1958. "Concession Agreements and Nationalization." *The American Journal of International Law* 52 (2): 260.

Castro-Gómez, Santiago, Oscar Guardiola-Rivera, and Carmen Millán de Benavides. 1999. "Introducción: Postcolonialismo, o la crítica cultural del capitalismo tardío." In *Los Intersticios: Teoría y práctica de la crítica poscolonial*, edited by Santiago Castro-Gómez, Oscar Guardiola-Rivera, and Carmen Millán de Benavides. Coleección Pensar.

Chacón-Lozsán, Francisco J. 2016. «Qué significa V.I.T.R.I.O.L.» *Masonería Libertaria.* 13 de Febrero. Último acceso: 16 de Enero de 2021. https://masonerialibertaria.com/2016/02/13/que-significa-v-i-t-r-i-o-l/.

Chakrabarty, Dipesh. 2000. *Downloaded Provincializing Europe: Postcolonial Thought and Historical Difference.* Princeton, NJ: Princeton University Press.

Chambers and Partners. n.d. "Arbitration – International – Globalwide." *Chamber and Partners.* Accessed June 15, 2020. http://www.chambersandpartners.com/15649/57/editorial/2/1.

Chang, Ha-Joon. 2003. *Kicking Away the Ladder: Development Strategy in Historical Perspective.* London: Anthem Press.

———. 2014. *Economics: The User's Guide.* London: Pelican.

Chanock, Martin. 1992. "The Law Market: The Legal Encounter in British East and Central Africa." In *European Expansion and Law: The Encounter of European Law in 19th- and 20th-Century Africa and Asia*, edited by W. J. Mommsen and J. A. De Moor, 59–82. Oxford: Oxford University Press.

Christie, George. 1962. "What Constitutes a Taking of Property Under International Law?" *British Year Book of International Law* 38: 307–338.

CMS Gas Transmission Company v. The Republic of Argentina. 2005. No. ARB/01/8 (ICSID Case).

Colangelo, Anthony J. 2016. "A Systems Theory of Fragmentation and Harmonization." *International Law and Politics* 49 (1): 1–61.

Colen, Liseth, and Andrea Guariso. 2013. "What Type of Foreign Direct Investment is Attracted by Bilateral Investment Treaties?" In *Foreign Direct Investment and Human Development: The Law and Economics of International Investment Agreements*, edited by Oliver de Schuteer, Johan Swinnen, and Jan Wouters, 138–156. London and New York: Routledge.

Colen, Liseth, Mi Maertens, and J. Swinnen. 1938. "Communication Sent by Codell Hull to the Government of Mexico, 5th of January 1929 in 'Mexico--United States: Expropriation by Mexico of Agrarian Properties Owned by American Citizens'." *The American Journal of International Law: Supplement Official Documents 181, 182* 32 (4).

———. 2013. "Foreign Direct Investment as an Engine for Economic Growth and Human Development." In *Foreign Direct Investment and Human Development: The Law and Economics of International Invetsment Agreements*, edited by Olivier de Schuteer, Johan Swinnen, and Jan Wouters, 70–115. London and New York: Routledge.

Compañia del Desarrollo de Santa Elena S.A. v. Republic of Costa Rica. 2000. No. ARB/96/1 (ICSID Case, February).

Connell, H. P. 1961. "United States Protection of Private Foreign Investment Through Treaties of Friendship, Commerce and Navigation." *H Archiv des Völkerrechts* 9 (3): 256–277.

Cornell, Drucilla. 2008. *Moral Images of Freedom: A Future for Critical Theory*. Lanham, MD: Rowman & Littlefield Publishers.

Coronil, Fernando. 2000. "Del Eurocentrsimo al Globocentrismo: La Naturaleza del Poscolonialismo." In *La Colonialidad del Saber: eurocentrismo y ciencias sociales, perspectivas latinoamericanas*, edited by Edgardo Lander. Buenos Aires: CLACSO-UNESCO.

D'Amato, Anthony. 2014. "Groundwork for International Law." *American Journal of International Law* 108 (4): 650–679.

D'Aspremont, Jean. 2014. "Send Back the Lifeboats: Confronting the Project of Saving International Law." *The American Journal of International Law* 108: 680–689.

Dautaj, Ylli, and Esmé Shirlow. 2020. "Kluwer Arbitration Blog." *The ICSID Reforms and Working Paper 4: Push or Pull?* March 14. Accessed October 6, 2020. http://arbitrationblog.kluwerarbitration.com/2020/03/14/the-icsid-reforms-and-working-paper-4-push-or-pull/.

Davis, Richard M. 1952. "The Current State of Profit Theory." *The American Economic Review* 42 (3): 245.

De Sousa Santos, Boaventura. 2002. *Towards a New Legal Common Sense*. London: Butherworths Lexis Nexis.

———. 2016. "A Critique of Lazy Reason: Against the Waste of Experience." In *The Modern World-System in the Longue Dureé*, edited by Immanuel Wallerstein. London: Routledge.

Deggau, Hans-Georg. 1988. "The Comunicative Autonomy of the Legal System." In *Autopoietic Law: A New Approach to Law and Society*, edited by Gaunther Teubner, 128–151. Berlin and New York: Walter de Gruyter.

Derrida, Jacques. 1995. *The Gift of the Death: And Literature in Secret*. Translated by David Wills. Chicago, IL: The University of Chicago Press.

Dolzer, Rudolph, and Christoph Schreuer. 2012. *Principles of International Investment Law*. New York: Oxford University Press.

Dolzer, Rudolf, and Feliz Bloch. 2003. "Indirect Expropriation: Conceptual Realignments?, (2003) (5) 155." *International Law FORUM du droit international* 5 (3): 155–165.

Dolzer, Rudolf, and Margrete Stewvens. 1995. *Bilateral Investment Treaties*. London: Martinus Nijhof Publishers.

Dupuy, Jean-Pierre. 1988. "On the Supposed Closure of Normative Systems." In *Autopoietic Law: A New Approach to Law and Society*, edited by Gunther Teubner, 51–69. Berlin and New York: Walter de Gruyter.

Dussel, Enrique. 1994. *1492 El Encubrimiento del Otro: Hacia el Origen del Mito de la Modernidad*. Plural Editores - Facultad de Humanidades y Ciencias de la Educación - UMSA.

———. 2014. *16 Tesis de Economía Política: Interpretación Filosófica*. México D.F.: Siglo Veintiuno Editores.

Egger, Petter, and Michael Pfaffermayr. 2009. "The Impact of Bilateral Investment Treaties on Foreign Direct Investment." In *The Effect of Treaties on Foreign Direct Investment: Bilateral Investment Treaties, Double Taxation Treaties and Investment Flows*, edited by Carl P. Sauvant and Lisa E. Sachs. Oxford: Oxford University Press.

Egger, Petter H., and Valeria Merlo. 2007. "The Impact of Bilateral Investment Treaties on FDI Dynamics." *The World Economy* 30 (10): 1536.

Elisa Van Wayenberge. n.d. "Tightening the Web: The World Bank and Enforced Policy Reform." In *The Rise and Fall of Neoliberalism: The Collapse of an Economic Order?*, edited by Kean Birch and Vlad Mykhnenko, 94. London: Zed Books 2010.

Elkins, Zachary, Andrew T. Guzman, and Beth A. Simmons. 2006. "Competing for Capital: The Diffusion of Bilateral Investment Treaties 1960–2000." *International Organization* 60: 811–846.

Enron Corporation and Ponderosa Assets, LP. v. Argentine Republic. 2007. No. ARB/01/3 (CSID Case).

Epstein, Richard A. 1985. *Takings: Private Property and The Power of Eminent Domain*. Cambridge: Harvard University Press.

Escobar, Arturo. 1995. *Encountering Development: The Making and Unmaking of the Third World*. Princeton, NJ: Princeton University Press.

European Commission. 2016. "The Multilateral Investment Court Project." *European Commission*. December 21. Accessed September 27, 2019. http://trade.ec.europa.eu/doclib/press/index.cfm?id=1608.

Falk, R. 1995. "Cultural Foundations for Protection of Human Rights." In *Human Rights in Cross-Cultural Perspective: A Quest for Consensus*, edited by Abdullahi Ahmed An-Nai´m. Philadelphia: University of Pennsylvania Press.

Fanon, Franz. 2004. *The Wretched of the Earth*. New York: Grove Press.

Farmer, Paul. 1996. "On Suffering and Structural Violence: A View from Below." *Daedalus* 125 (1): 261.

Faundez, Julio, and Celine Tan. 2010. "Introduction." In *International Economic Law, Globalization and Developing Countries*, edited by Julio Faundez and Celine Tan, 1–9. Northampton, MA: Edward Elgar.

Fine, Ben. 2009. "Development as Zombieconomics in the Age of Neoliberalism." *Third World Quarterly* 30 (5): 885.

Fisher, Anthony. 1978. *Fisher's Concise History of Economic Bungling: A Guide for Today's Statesmen*. Ottowa: Caroline House.

Forbes. 2013. "Emerging Markets: Joining The Global Ranks Of Wealth Creators." *Forbes Insight*. Accessed November 24, 2020. http://images.forbes.com/forbesinsights/StudyPDFs/SocieteGenerale-Emerging_Markets-Report.pdf.

Foucault, Michele. 1972. *The Archaeology of Knowledge & the Discourse on Language.* Translated by A. M. Sheridan Smith. New York: Pantheon Books.

———. 2008a. *The Birth of Biopolitics: Lectures at the College De France, 1978–1979.* Edited by Michel Senellart. Translated by Graham Burchell. New York: Palgrave Macmillan.

———. 2008b. *The Birth of Biopolitics: Lectures at the College De France, 1978–1979.* Translated by Graham Burchell. New York: Palgrave Macmillan.

Franck, Susan D. 2007. "Empirically Evaluating Claims About Investment Treaty Arbitration." *North Carolina Law Review* 96 (1): 1–87.

———. 2007–2008. "Empirically Evaluating Claims About Investment Treaty Arbitration." *North Carolina Law Review* 86: 29.

Frank, Andre Gunder. 2009. *Capitalism and Underdevelopment in Latin America Historical Studies of Chile and Brazil.* New York and London: Monthly Review Press.

Fraser, Henry S. 1926. "Sketch of the History of International Arbitration." *Cornell Law Review* 11 (2): 179.

Freud, Sigmund. 1919. "The 'Uncanny'." Accessed September 5, 2020. http://web.mit.edu/allanmc/www/freud1.pdf.

Frost, Gerald. 2008. *Antony Fisher: Champion of Liberty.* Accessed September 25, 2020. https://iea.org.uk/publications/research/antony-fisher-champion-of-liberty.

Galtung, Johan. 1969. "Violence, Peace, and Peace Research." *Journal of Peace Research* 6 (3): 167–191.

Gary Gutting. 2007. "Introduction Michel Foucault: A User's Manual." In *The Cambridge Companion to Foucault*, edited by Gary Gutting. Cambridge, MA: Cambridge University Press.

Gerber, David J. 1994. "Constitutionalizing the Economy: German Neo-Liberalism, Competition Law and the "New" Europe." *The American Journal of Comparative Law* 42: 25–84.

Gilgen, Peter. 2013. "System—Autopoiesis-Form: An Introduction to Luhmann's Introduction to Systems Theory." In *Introduction to Systems Theory*, edited by Niklas Luhman, xi. Cambridge: Polity Press.

Global Affairs Canada. 2018. "Canada's Foreign Investment Promotion and Protection Agreements." *Global Affairs Canada.* Accessed October 16, 2020. https://www.international.gc.ca/trade-commerce/consultations/fipa-apie/index.aspx?lang=eng.

Göçer, İsmet, Mehmet Mercan, and Osman Peker. 2014. "Effect of Foreign Direct Investments on the Domestic Investments of Developing Countries: A Dynamic Panel Data Analysis." *Journal of Economic and Social Studies* 4 (1): 73.

Goldreich, Oded. 2004. *Foundations of Cryptography Basic Tools.* Cambridge: Cambridge University Press.

Goodrich, Peter. 1987. *Legal Discourse: Studies in Linguistic, Rhetoric and Legal Analysis.* London: Palgrave Macmillan.

Gordon, Jane Anna. 2006. "Some Reflections on Challenges Posed to Social Scientific Method by the Study of Race." In *A Companion to African-American Studies*, edited by Lewis R. Gordon and Jane Anna Gordon. Malden, MA: Blackwell.

Gordon, Lewis. 2015. *Disciplinary Decadence: Living Thought in Trying Times*. London: Routledge.

Gordon, Lewis R. 2006. "Africana Thought and African-Diasporic Studies." In *A Companion to African-American Studies*, edited by Lewis R. Gordon and Jane Anna Gordon. Malden, MA: Blackwell.

———. 2015. *What Fanon Said: A Philosophical Introduction to His Life and Thought*. London: Hurst & Company.

———. 2017. "Frantz Fanon." In *Histories Of Violence: Post-War Critical Thought*, edited by Brad Evans and Terrell Carver. London: Zed Books.

Gordon, Lewis R., and Jane Anna Gordon. 2006. *A Companion to African-American Studies*. Malden, MA: Blackwell.

Greider, William. 2001. *The Right and US Trade Law: Invalidating the 20th Century*. November 17. Accessed July 2020. https://www.thenation.com/article/archive/right-and-us-trade-law-invalidating-20th-century/.

Guardiola-Rivera, Oscar. 2010. *What If Latin America Rule the World? How the South Will Take the North into the 22nd Century*. London: Bloomsbury.

———. 2013. *Story of a Death Foretold: The Coup Against Salvador Allende, 11 September 1973*. London: Bloomsbury.

Gunder, Michael. 2010. "Planning as the Ideology of (Neoliberal) Space." *Planning Theory* 9 (4): 298–314.

Hallward-Driemeier, Mary. 2009. "Do Bilateral Investment Treaties Attract FDI? Only a Bit…and They Could Bite." In *The Effect of Treaties on Foreign Direct Investment: Bilateral Investment Treaties, Double Taxation Treaties*, edited by Carl P. Sauvant and Lisa E. Sachs. Oxford: Oxford University Press.

Harnik, Andrew. 2020. "Big Finance, Big Tech and Joe Biden." *The New York Times*, August 10.

Harten, Gus Van. 2007. *Investment Treaty Arbitration and Public Law*. Oxford: Oxford University Press.

———. 2008a. "A Case for an International Investment Court." *Working Paper Society of International Economic Law* 22 (8).

———. 2008b. "A Case for an International Investment Court." *All Papers*. July 16. Accessed June 12, 2020. https://digitalcommons.osgoode.yorku.ca/cgi/viewcontent.cgi?article=1258&context=all_papers.

———. 2008c. "A Case for an International Investment Court." *Osgoode Digital Commons*. July 15. Accessed September 27, 2019. https://digitalcommons.osgoode.yorku.ca/cgi/viewcontent.cgi?referer=https://www.google.com/&httpsredir=1&article=1258&context=all_papers.

———. 2013. *Sovereign Choices and Sovereign Constraints*. Oxford: Oxford University Press.

Harten, Gus Van, and Dayna Nadine Scott. 2016. "Investment Treaties and the Internal Vetting of Regulatory Proposals: A Case Study from Canada." *Osgoode Legal Studies Research Paper Series* 151.

———. 2017. "Investment Treaties and the Internal Vetting of Regulatory Proposals: A Case Study from Canada." *International Institute for Sustainable Development*. September 20. Accessed November 10, 2020. https://www.iisd.org/itn/en/2017/09

/26/investment-treaties-internal-vetting-regulatory-proposals-case-study-from-canada-gus-van-harten-dayna-nadine-scott/.

Hathaway, Oona A., and Scott J. Shapiro. 2017. *The Internationalist and Their Plan to Outlaw War.* London: Allen Lane.

Hayek, Friedrich. 1947. *Professor Friedrich Hayek's Closing Speech.* Accessed September 25, 2020. http://fc95d419f4478b3b6e5f-3f71d0fe2b653c4f00f32175760e96e7.r87.cf1.rackcdn.com/FF1AB6C707734EA895EC45EEC417D3F8.pdf.

Heron, Taitu. 2008. "Neoliberalism and the Exercise of Human Agency." *International Journal of Politics, Culture, and Society* 20 (1/4): 85–101.

Hinojosa, Leonith, and Anthony Bebbington. 2010. "Transnational Companies and Transnational Civil Society." In *The Rise and Fall of Neoliberalism: The Collapse of an Economic Order?*, edited by Kean Birch and Vlad Mykhnenko. London: Zed Books.

Ho, Kathleen. 2007. "Structural Violence as a Human Rights Violation." *Essex Human Rights Review* 4 (2): 1–17.

Houde, Marie-France. 2006. "OECD." *Novel Features in Recent OECD Bilateral Investment Treaties.* Accessed October 6, 2020. http://www.oecd.org/investment/internationalinvestmentagreements/40072428.pdf.

ICSID. 2018. "Backgrounder on Proposals for Amendment of the ICSID Rules." *ICSID.* August 3. Accessed September 27, 2019. https://icsid.worldbank.org/en/Documents/Amendment_Backgrounder.pdf.

———. 2020. "International Centre for Settlemento of Investmennt Disputes." *Proposals for Amendments of the ICSID Rules - Working Paper # 4.* February. Accessed September 26, 2020. https://icsid.worldbank.org/sites/default/files/WP_4_Vol_1_En.pdf.

International Institute for Sustainable Development. 2017. "UNCITRAL and Reform of Investment Dispute Settlement." *International Institute for Sustainable Development.* July. Accessed October 6, 2020. https://www.iisd.org/projects/uncitral-and-reform-investment-dispute-settlement.

———. 2019. "Summary Comments to the Proposals for Amendment of the ICSID Arbitration Rules." *International Institute for Sustainable Development.* March 15. Accessed September 27, 2019. https://icsid.worldbank.org/en/Documents/IISD.pdf.

International Law Commission. 2001. *Draft Articles on Responsibility of States for Internationally Wrongful Acts, With Commentaries.* United Nations.

Isakoff, Peter D. 2013. "Defining the Scope of Indirect Expropriation for International Investments." *Global Business Law Review* 3 (2): 189.

Jacobson, Arthur J. 1989. "Autopoietic Law: The New Science of Niklas Luhmann." *Michigan Law Review* 87 (6): 1647–1689.

Johnson, Lise. 2012. "Columbia Center on Sustainable Investment." *The 2012 US Model BIT and What the Changes (or Lack Thereof) Suggest About Future Investment Treaties.* November. Accessed October 16, 2020. http://ccsi.columbia.edu/files/2014/01/johnson_2012usmodelBIT.pdf.

Kapeliuk, Daphna. 2010. "The Repeat Appointment Factor: Exploring Decision Patterns of Elite Investment Arbitrators." *Cornell Law Review* 96 (1): 47–90.

Kaushal, Asha. 2009. "Revisiting History: How the Past Matters for the Present Backlash Against the Foreign Investment Regime." *Harvard International Law Journal* 50 (2): 491.

Keith Aoki. 1998. "Neocolonialism, Anticommons Property, and Biopiracy in the (Not-so-Brave) New World Order of International Intellectual Property Protection." *Indiana Journal of Global Legal Studies* 6 (1): 11.

Kennedy, Emmet. 1979. "'Ideology' from Destutt De Tracy to Marx." *Journal of the History of Ideas* 40 (3): 353–358.

Koopman, Colin. 2013. *Genealogy as Critique: Foucault and the Problems of Modernity.* Bloomington: Indiana University Press.

Koskenniemi, Martti. 2006. *Fragmentation of International Law: Difficulties Arising from the Diversification and Expansion of International Law.* Report of the Study Group of the International Law Commission, International Law Commission. Geneva: International Law Commission.

Ladeur, Karl-Heinz. 1999. "The Theory of Autopoiesis as an Approach to a Better Understanding of Postmodern Law." *European University Institute Working Paper 99/3* (European University Institute, Florence Department of Law EUI Working Paper LAW No. 99/3 The Theory of Autopoiesis as an Approach to a Better Understanding of Postmodern Law From the Hierarchy of Norms to the Heterarchy of Changing Patterns of Legal Inter) 1–45.

Landau, Susan. 2004. "Polynomials in the Nation's Service: Using Algebra to Design the Advanced Encryption Standard." *The American Mathematical Monthly* 111 (2): 89–117.

Lander, Edgardo. 2000. "Ciencias Sociales: Saberes Coloniales y Eurocentricos." In *La Colonialidad del Saber: eurocentrismo y ciencias sociales, perspectivas latinoamericanas*, edited by Edgardo Lander. Buenos Aires: CLACSO-UNESCO.

Lang, Andrew. 2011. *World Trade Law after Neoliberalism: Reimagining the Global Economic Order.* Oxford: Oxford University Press.

Langford, Malcolm. 2019. "UNCITRAL and Investment Arbitration Reform: A Little More Action." *Kluwer Arbitration Blog.* October 21. Accessed October 6, 2020. http://arbitrationblog.kluwerarbitration.com/2019/10/21/uncitral-and-investment-arbitration-reform-a-little-more-action/.

Langford, Malcolm, Daniel Behn, and Runar Hilleren Lie. 2017. "The Revolving Door in International Investment Arbitration." *Journal of International Economic Law* 20: 301–331.

Lapavistas, Costas. 2005. "Mainstream Economic in the Neoliberal Era." In *Neoliberalism a Critical Reader*, edited by Alfredo Saad and Deborah Johnston. Ann Arbor: Pluto Press.

Levine, Eugenia. 2011. "Amicus Curiae in International Investment Arbitration: The Implications of an Increase in Third Party Participation." *Berkeley Journal of International Law* 29 (1): 200.

LEXICO. n.d. *LEXICO.* Accessed June 4, 2020. https://www.lexico.com/definition/violence.

LG & Energy Corp., LG&E Capital Corp. and LG&E International, Inc. v. Argentine Republic. 2008. No. ARB/02/1 (CSID Case).

Linden, Harry van der. 2012. "On the Violence of Systemic Violence: A Critique of Slavoj Žižek." *Radical Philosophy Review* 15 (1): 33–51.

Link-Trading Joint Stock Company v. Department for Customs Control of the Republic of Moldova. 2002. (UNCITRAL).

Lipson, Charles. 1985. *Standing Guard: Protecting Foreign Capital in the Nineteenth and Twentieth Century*. California: University of California Press.

Liseth Colen, Miet Maertens, and Johan Swinnen. 2013. "Foreign Direct Investment as an Engine for Economic Growth and Human Development." In *Foreign Direct Investment and Human Development: The Law and Economics of International Agreements*, edited by Oliver Schutter, Johan Swinnen, and Jan Wouters, 70–115. Abindgon: Routledge.

Locke, John. 1690. "An Essay Concerning the True Original, Extent and End of Civil Government: On Government: Chapter 11." *American History*. Accessed June 29, 2020. http://www.let.rug.nl/usa/documents/1651-1700/john-locke-essay-on-government/chapter-11-of-the-extent-of-the-legislative-power.php.

Luhman, Niklas. 1988a. "Closure and Openness: On Reality in the World of Law." In *Autopoietic Law: A New Approach to Law and Society*, edited by Gunther Teubner, 335–348. Berlin and New York: Walter de Gruyter.

———. 1988b. "The Unity of the Legal System." In *Autopoietic Law: A New Approach to Law and Society*, edited by Gunther Teubner, 12–35. Berlin; New York: Walter de Gruyter.

———. 2013. *Introduction to Systems Theory*. Cambridge, MA: Polity Press.

Mäki, Uskali. 2009. *The Methodology of Positive Economics : Reflections on the Milton Friedman Legacy*. Cambridge, MA: Cambridge University Press.

Malmström, Cecilia. 2015. *European Commission*. September 16. Accessed September 27, 2019. https://ec.europa.eu/commission/commissioners/2014-2019/malmstrom/blog/proposing-investment-court-system_en.

Manhattan Forums. n.d. *Manhattan Forums, the First Five Years*. Accessed September 25, 2020. https://media4.manhattan-institute.org/pdf/mi_five.pdf.

Marks, Susan. 2003. *The Riddle of All Constitutions: International Law, Democracy and the Critique of Ideology*. Oxford: Oxford University Press.

Martti, Koskenniemi. 2009. "The Politics of International Law." *The European Journal of International Law* 20 (1): 7–19.

Mattei, Ugo, and Laura Nader. 2008. *Plunder: When the Rule of Law Is Illegal*. Oxford: Blackwell Publishing.

McCloskey, Deirdre N. 1995. *The Rhetoric of Economics*. Madison: The University of Wisconsin Press.

McSwain, Cynthia J., Jr. Orion F. White, and Willa Bruce. 1989. "Transforming the Golem: Technicism, Human-Relations Technology, and the Human." *Public Administration Review* 49 (2): 197–200.

Mendez Hincapíe, Gabriel, and Ricardo Sanín-Restrepo. 2012. "La Constitución Encriptada: Nuevas formas de emancipación del poder global." *Revista de Derechos Humanos y Estudios Sociales* 9: 97–120.

Mendieta, Eduardo. 2011. "The Ethics of (Not) Knowing: The Care of Ethics and Knowledge Will Come of Its Own Accord." In *Decolonizing Epistemologies:*

Latina/o Theology and Philosophy, edited by Ada Maria Isasi-Diaz and Eduardo Mendieta. New York: Fordahm University Press.

———. 2015. "Globalization, Cosmopolitics, Decoloniality: Politics for/of the Anthropocene." In *Bloomsbury Companion to Political Philosophy*, edited by Andrew Fiala. London: Bloomsbury.

Metalclad Corporation v. The United Mexican States. 2000. No. ARB(AF)/97/1 (ICSID Case, August).

Miles, Kate. 2010. "International Investment Law: Origins, Imperialism and Conceptualizing the Environment." *Colorado Journal of International Environmental Law and Policy* 21 (1): 1.

———. 2013. *The Origins of International Investment Law: Empire, Environment and the Safeguard of Capital*. Cambridge: Cambridge University Press.

Miller, David. 2010. "How Neoliberalism Got Where It Is: Elite Planning, Corporate Lobbying and the Release of the Free Market." In *The Rise and Fall of Neoliberalism: The Collapse of an Economic Order?*, edited by Kean Birch and Vlad Mykhnenko. London: Zed Books.

MINCIT (Colombian Ministry of Industry, Commerce and Tourism). 2017. "BIT Model (Bilateral Investment Treaty between the Republic of Colombia and)." *MINCIT*. Accessed October 16, 2020. https://www.mincit.gov.co/temas-interes/documentos/model-bit-2017.aspx.

Monica, Paul R. La. 2017. "The Biggest Winners and Losers from Trumponomics." January 18. Accessed November 24, 2020. https://money.cnn.com/2017/01/18/investing/donald-trump-corporate-america-domestic-sales/index.html?iid=SF_River.

Mostafa, Ben. 2008a. "The Sole Effects Doctrine, Police Powers and Indirect Expropriation Under International Law." *Australian International Law Journal* 15: 268–296.

———. 2008b. "The Sole Effects Doctrine, Police Powers and Indirect Expropriation Under International Law." *Australian International Law Journal* 15: 267.

Mudge, Stephanie Lee. 2008. "What is Neoliberalism?" *Socio Economic Review* 6 (4): 703–731.

Murad, Anatol. 1951. "An Uncertainty Theory of Profit: Comment." *The American Economic Review* 41 (1): 164.

Neumann, Franz, Herbert Marcuse, and Otto Kirchheimer. 2013. *Secret Reports on Nazi Germany: The Frankfurt School Contribution to the War Effort*. Edited by Raffaele Laudani. Princeton, NJ: Princeton University Press.

Neumayer, Erik, and Laura Spess. 2005. "Do Bilateral Investment Treaties Increase Foreign Direct Investment to Developing Countries." *World Development* 33 (10): 1567.

Newman, Graeme R. 1971. *Understanding Violence*. New York: J. P. Lippincott.

Newyork Times. 1997. *Aron Broches, 83, Official at World Bank*. September 19. Accessed November 4, 2020.

Nielsen, Lynge. 2011. "Classifications of Countries Based on Their Level of Development: How It Is Done and How It Could Be Done." *International Monetary Fund*. February. Accessed November 24, 2020. https://www.imf.org/external/pubs/ft/wp/2011/wp1131.pdf.

Ninth International Conference of American States. 1948. "Economic Agreement of Bogota." *OAS*. February 5. Accessed June 29, 2020. http://www.oas.org/juridico/english/sigs/a-43.html.

Nkrumah, Kwame. 1965. *Neo-Colonialism: The Last Stage of Imperialism*. London: Thomas Nelson Ltd.

Occidental Petroleum Corporation and Occidental Exploration and Production Company v. The Republic of Ecuador. 2012. ARB/06/11 (ICSID, October 12).

———. 2015. ARB/06/11 (ICSID, November 2).

Odumosu, Ibironke T. 2006–2007. "The Antinomies of the (Continued) Relevance of ICSID to the Third World." *San Diego International Law Journal* 8: 345.

OECD. 1967. "Draft Convention on the Protection of Foreign Property." *OECD*. Accessed June 28, 2020. http://www.oecd.org/dataoecd/35/4/39286571.pdf.

———. 2004. "Most Favoured Nation Treatment in International Investment Law - Working Papers on International Investment." *OECD*. Sptember. Accessed June 28, 2020. https://www.oecd.org/daf/inv/investment-policy/WP-2004_2.pdf.

Office of the Spokesperson US Department of State. 2012. "Model Bilateral Investment Treaty - Fact Sheet." *US Department of State*. April 20. Accessed October 16, 2020. https://2009-2017.state.gov/r/pa/prs/ps/2012/04/188199.htm.

Office of the United States Trade Representative. 2012. "2012 U.S. Model Bilateral Investment Treaty." *Office of the United States Trade Representative*. Accessed October 16, 2020. https://ustr.gov/sites/default/files/BIT%20text%20for%20ACIEP%20Meeting.pdf.

Olivet, Cecilia, Bettina Müller, and Luciana Ghiotto. 2017. "Impacts of Investment Arbitration Against Latin America and the Caribbean: ISDS in Numbers." *Transnational Institute*. December 11. Accessed October 18, 2020. https://www.tni.org/en/publication/impacts-of-investment-arbitration-against-latin-america-and-the-caribbean.

———. n.d. *ORDO Journal*. Accessed June 2, 2020. http://www.ordo-jahrbuch.de/de/index.html.

Pahuja, Sundhya. 2008. "Decolonising International Law: Development, Economic Growth and the Politics Of Universality." *Thesis Submitted for the Degree of Doctor of Philosophy Birkbeck University of London*. London: Thesis Submitted for the Degree of Doctor of Philosophy Birkbeck University of London.

———. 2011. *Decolonising International Law: Development, Economic Growth and the Politics of Universality*. Cambridge: Cambridge University Press.

Pakistan and Federal Republic of Germany Treaty for the Promotion and Protection of Investments. 1959. *Pakistan and Federal Republic of Germany Treaty for the Promotion and Protection of Investments*. Vol. 6575. Bonn: The United Nations, November 25.

Palma, Gabriel. 1981. "Dependency and Development: A Critical Overview." In *Dependency Theory: A Critical Reassessment*, edited by Dudley Seers. London: Francer Pinter Publishers.

Patnaik, Utsa. 1999. "EMS on the Agrarian Question: Ground Rent and Its Implications." *Social Scientist* 27 (9): 51.

Pecheux, Michel. 1982. *Language, Semantics and Ideology: Stating the Obvious.* Translated by Harbans Nagpal. London: The MacMillan Press Ltd.

Peck, Jamie. 2008. "Remaking Laissez-Faire." *Progress in Human Geography* 32 (1): 3–43.

———. 2012. *Constructions of Neoliberal Reason.* Oxford: Oxford University Press.

Peck, Jamie, and Adam Tickell. 2002. "Neoliberalizing Space." *Antipode* 343 (3): 380.

Perrone, Nicolás. 2016. "The International Investment Regime After the Global Crisis of Neoliberalism: Rupture or Continuity?" *Indiana Journal of Global Legal Studies* 23 (2): 603.

Perry-Kessaris, Amanda. 2008. *Global Business Local Law: The Indian Legal System as a Communal Resource in Foreign Investment Relations.* Aldershot: Ashgate.

Peterson, Luke Eric, and Kevin R Gray. 2003. *International Human Rights in Bilateral Investment Treaties and in Investment Treaty Arbitration.* Working Paper, International Institute for Sustainable Development (IISD).

Philip Morris Brands Sàrl, Philip Morris Products S.A. and Abal Hermanos S.A. v. Oriental Republic of Uruguay (formerly FTR Holding SA, Philip Morris Products S.A. and Abal Hermanos S.A. v. Oriental Republic of Uruguay). 2016. No. ARB/10/7 (ICSID Case, July).

Philippopoulos-Mihalopoulos, Andreas. 2014. "Critical Autopoiesis and the Materiality of Law." *International Journal for the Semiotics of Law* 27: 389–418.

Piketty, Thomas. 2014. *Capital in the Twenty-First Century.* Translated by Arthur Goldhammer. Harvard: Belknap Harvard.

Pilkington, Ed. 2016. *Leaked Documents Reveal Secretive Influence of Corporate Cash on Politics.* September 14. Accessed June 2020. https://www.theguardian.com/us-news/2016/sep/14/corporate-cash-john-doe-files-scott-walker-wisconsin.

Prieto-Rios, Enrique. 2015. "Neoliberal Market Rationality: The Driver of International Investment Law." *Birkbeck Law Review* 3 (1): 55–76.

———. 2018. "Encrypted International Investment Law in the Age of Neo-Colonialism." In *Decrypting Power*, edited by Ricardo Sanín-Restrepo, 49–66. London: Rowman & Littlefield.

Prieto-Rios, Enrique, Andrei Gómez-Suarez, and Nicloás M Perrone. 2016. "Foreign Investors adn the Colombian Peace Process." *International Community Law Review* (18): 223–247.

Prieto-Rios, Enrique, Andrés Gómez-Rey, and Mariana Diaz-Chalela. 2019. "Betweenn the Environment and Foreign Investment Protection: The Case of Santurban in ICSID." In *Crisis del EstadoNación y de la Concepción Clásica de la Soberanía*, edited by Manuel Alberto Restrepo Medina, 161–190. Bogotá: Editorial Universidad del Rosario.

Prieto-Rios, Enrique, and Daniel Rivas. 2020. "Neocolonialism and the Tension Between International Investment Law and Indigenous Peoples: The Latin American Experience." In *Indigenous Peoples and International Trade*, edited by John Borrows and Risa Schwartz. Cambridge: Cambridge University Press.

Prieto-Rios, Enrique, and Kojo Koram. 2015. "Decolonising Epistemologies, Politicising Rights: An Interview with Eduardo Mendieta." *Birkbeck Law Review* 3 (1): 13–31.

Prieto-Rios, Enrique, and Rene Urueña. 2017. "Colombia: un Estado bipolar en materia de inversión extranjera." *Razón Pública*. July 31. Accessed October 17, 2020. https://razonpublica.com/colombia-un-estado-bipolar-en-materia-de-inversion-extranjera/.

Puig, Sergio. 2014. "Social Capital in the Arbitration Market." *The European Journal of International Law* 25 (2): 387–424.

Quijano, Anibal. 2000. "Colonialidad del Poder, Eurocentrismo y América Latina." In *La Colonialidad del Saber: eurocentrismo y ciencias sociales, perspectivas latinoamericanas*, edited by Edgardo Lander. Buenos Aires: CLACSO-UNESCO.

Quiles, Nicolás. 2011. «Los espejos. Grandes maestros que descubren nuestro interior.» *Masoneria y Simbolismo*. 6 de Octubre. Último acceso: 17 de Enero de 2021. http://masoneriaysimbolismo.blogspot.com/2011/10/los-espejos-grandes-maestros-que.html.

Rabaka, Reiland. 2016. "The Weapon of Critical Theory: Amilcar Cabral, Cabralism, and Africana Critical Theory." In *Resistance and Decolonozation*, edited by Amilcar Cabral, 1–42. Lanham, MD: Rowman & Littlefield.

Rahimi, Sadeq. 2013. "The Ego, the Ocular, and the Uncanny: Why Are Metaphors of Vision Central in Accounts of the Uncanny?" *The International Journal of Psychoanalysis* 94: 453–476.

Ranjan, Prabhash, and Pushkar Anand. 2017. "The 2016 Model Indian Bilateral Investment Treaty: A Critical Deconstruction." *Northwestern Journal of International Law & Business* 38: 1–54.

Rist, Gilbert. 2008. *The History of Development: From Western Origins to Global Faith*. London: Zed Books.

Roberts, Anthea. 2013. "Clash of Paradigms: Actors and Analogies Shaping the Investment Treaty System." *The American Journal of International Law* 107 (1): 45–94.

Rogers, Catherine A. 2014. "The Politics of International Investment Arbitrators." *Santa Clara Journal of International Law* 12 (1): S223.

Root, Elihu. 1910. "The Basis of Protection to Citizens Residing Abroad." *The American Journal of International Law* 4 (3): 517.

Rosenfeld, Michel. 1991. "Autopoiesis and Justice." *Cardozo Law Review*: 1681–1712.

Rottleuthner, Hubert. 1988. "Biological Metaphors in Legal Thought." In *Autopoietic Law: A New Approach to Law and Society*, edited by Gunther Teubner, 97–127. Berlin and New York: Walter de Gruyter.

Rouse, Joseph. 2007. "Power/Knowledge." In *The Cambridge Companion to Foucault*, edited by Gary Gutting, 95–122. Cambridge: Cambridge University Press.

Saad-Filho, Alfredo. 2005. "Development, from Washington to Post-Washington Consensus: Neoliberal Agendas for Economic Development." In *Neoliberalism a Critical Reader*, edited by Alfredo Saad-Filho and Deborah Johnston, 113–119. London: Pluto Press.

Said, Edward W. 2007. *Orientalism*. London: Penguin.
Salacuse, Jeswald W., and Nicholas P. Sullivan. 2009. "Do BITs Really Work?: An Evaluation of Bilateral Investment Treaties and Their Grand Bargain." In *The Effect of Treaties on Foreign Direct Investment: Bilateral Investment Treaties, Double Taxation Treaties and Investment Flows*, edited by Carl P. Sauvant and Lisa E. Sachs. Oxford: Oxford University Press.
Saluka Investments B.V. v. The Czech Republic. 2005. Partial Award (UNCITRAL).
Sánchez Lissen, Rocío. 2005. *Juan Sardá y La Política Monetaria Del Plan De Estabilización*. Accessed September 25, 2020. http://www.usc.es/estaticos/congresos/histec05/b1_sanchez_lissen.pdf.
Sauvy, Alfred. 1952. "Trois Mondes, Une Planète." *Le Magazine del'homme moderne*. Accessed November 4, 2020. http://www.homme-moderne.org/societe/demo/sauvy/3mondes.html.
Schill, Stephan W. 2006. "Fair and Equitable Treatment Under Investment Treaties as an Embodiment of the Rule of Law." *International Law and Justice Working Papers - Global Administrative Law Series 2* 6.
———. 2009. *The Multilateralization of International Investment Law*. Cambridge: Cambridge University Press.
———. 2010a. "International Investment Law and Comparative Public Law: An Introduction." In *International Investment Law and Comparative Public Law*, edited by Stephan W. Schill. Oxford University Press.
———. 2010b. "Umbrella Clauses as Public Law Concepts in Comparative Perspective." In *International Investment Law and Comparative Public Law*, edited by Stephan W. Schill, 318. Oxford: Oxford University Press.
Schneiderman, David. 2010. "Judicial Politics and International Investment Arbitration: Seeking an Explanation for Conflicting Outcomes." *Northwestern Journal of International Law & Business* 30 (1): 383–416.
———. 2013. *Resisting Economic Globalization: Critical Theory and International Investment Law*. New York: Palgrave Macmillan.
Schultz, Thomas. 2011. "Editorial Arbitration as an iPhone, or Why Conduct Academic Research in Arbitration?" *Journal of International Dispute Settlement* 2 (2): 279–286.
Schwartz, Pedro. 1997. *El País*. July 11. Accessed September 10, 2020. https://elpais.com/diario/1997/07/12/economia/868658415_850215.html.
SGS Société Générale de Surveillance S.A. v. Islamic Republic of Pakistan. 2003. No. ARB/01/13 (ICSID Case).
Silva, Patricio. 2006. "The Politic of Neoliberalism in Latin America: Legitimacy, Depoliticization and Technocratic Rule in Chile." In *The Neo-Liberal Revolution: Forging the Market State*, edited by Richard Robinson. New York: Palgrave MacMillan.
Silver, Caleb. 2020. *Investopedia*. March 18. Accessed June 5, 2020. https://www.investopedia.com/insights/worlds-top-economies/.
Simons, Henry Calvet. 1948. *Economic Policy for a Free Society*. Chicago, IL: University of Chicago Press.

Smith, Adam. 2007. "An Inquiry into the Nature and Causes of the Wealth of Nations (Books I, II, III, IV and V)." *Ibiblio.* May 29. Accessed May 2020. https://www.ibiblio.org/ml/libri/s/SmithA_WealthNations_p.pdf.

Söderman, Martin. 2020. "India's 2016 Model Bilateral Investment Treaty: A Backlash to the Calvo Doctrine and Legal Nationalism?" *Stockholms Universitet.* Accessed October 17, 2020. https://su.diva-portal.org/smash/get/diva2:1454640/FULLTEXT01.pdf.

Sornarajah, M. 2010. *The International Law on Foreign Investment.* Cambridge: Cambridge University Press.

———. 2011. "Mutations of Neo-Liberalism in International Investment Law." *Trade Law and Development* 3 (1): 203–231.

———. 2017. *The International Law on Foreign Investment.* Cambridge, MA: Cambridge University Press.

Stiglitz, Joseph E. 1999. "The World Bank at the Millennium." *The Economic Journal* 109 (459): F577–F597.

Subhashini, Ali. 2002. "Neocolonialism at Ground Zero: Globalization and Poor Women in India." *New Labour Forum* 11: 29.

Suk, Jeannie. 2008. "Taking the Home." *Law and Literature* 20 (3): 291–317.

Swamy, M. R. Kumara. 2011. "Are Multinational Corporations Problem-Solver or Problem-Makers in Developing Countries? Focus on Technology Gap and Arbitrage." *International Journal of Business* 16 (1): 72.

Szkorupova, Zuzana. 2015. "Relationship Between Foreign Direct Investment and Domestic Investment in Selected Countries of Central and Eastern Europe." *Procedia Economics and Finance* 23: 1017.

Técnicas Medioambientales Tecmed, S.A. v. United Mexican States. 2003. No. ARB(AF)/00/2 (ICSID Case).

Teubner, Gunther. 1941. *The Atlantic Charter: Declaration of Principles Issued by the President of the United States and the Prime Minister of the United Kingdom.* August 14. Accessed February 6, 2020. https://www.nato.int/cps/en/natolive/official_texts_16912.htm.

———. 1988a. "Evolution of Autopoietic Law." In *Autopoietic Law: A New Approach to Law and Society,* edited by Gunther Teubner, 217–241. Berlin and New York: Walter de Gruyter.

———. 1988b. "Introduction to Autopoietic Law." In *Autopoietic Law: A New Approach to Law and Society,* edited by Gunther Teubner, 1. Berlin and New York: Walter de Gruyter.

The World Bank. 2019. *GDP.* Accessed June 5, 2020. https://data.worldbank.org/indicator/NY.GDP.MKTP.CD.

———. n.d.a. *GDP.* Accessed June 5, 2020. https://data.worldbank.org/indicator/NY.GDP.MKTP.CD.

———. n.d.b. "How Does the World Bank Classify Countries?" *The World Bank.* Accessed November 24, 2020. https://datahelpdesk.worldbank.org/knowledgebase/articles/378834-how-does-the-world-bank-classify-countries.

The World Bank Group. 1992a. *Report to the Development Committee and Guidelines on the Treatment of Foreign Direct Investment.* The World Bank, Volume III.

———. 1992b. "Report to the Development Committee and Guidelines on the Treatment of Foreign Investors. Volume II." *World Bank.* Accessed June 30, 2020. http://documents1.worldbank.org/curated/en/955221468766167766/pdf/multi-page.pdf.

Tienhaara, K. 2006a. "What You Don't Know Can Hurt You: Investor-State Disputes and the Protection of the Environment in Developing Countries." *Global Environmental Politics* 6: 183.

———. 2006b. "What You Don't Know Can Hurt You: Investor-State Disputes and the Protection of the Environment in Developing Countries." *Global Environmental Politics* 6 (4): 73–100.

Titi, Catharine. 2013. "The Evolving BIT: A Commentary on Canada's Model Agreement." *IISD.* June 26. Accessed October 16, 2020. https://www.iisd.org/itn/fr/2013/06/26/the-evolving-bit-a-commentary-on-canadas-model-agreement/.

Tlostanova, Madina, and Walter Mignolo. 2009. "Global Coloniality and the Decolonial Option." *Kult* (6): 130.

Torre, Lisandro de la. 6012 (v.·.l.·.). «Parvis (o pasos perdidos).» *Respetable Logia Libertadores No.434.* 19 de Septiembre. Último acceso: 16 de Enero de 2021. https://logialibertadoresblog.wordpress.com/parvis-o-pasos-perdidos/#:~:text=El%20%E2%80%9Cparvis%E2%80%9D%20de%20un%20Templo,la%20reuni%C3%B3n%20de%20los%20HH%3A.&text=Mas%C3%B3nicamente%20al%20%E2%80%9Cparvis%E2%80%9D%20se%20lo,Templo%20y.

Tostanova, Madlina, and Walter Mignolo. 2009. "Global Coloniality and the Decolonial Option' Epistemologies of Transformation: The Latin American Decolonial Option and Its Ramifications." *Kultur (Special Issue: Epistemologies of Transformation)* 6: 130–147.

Treaty for the Promotion and Protection of Investments (with Protocol and exchange of notes) Pakistan and Federal Republic of Germany. 1959. (November 25).

Truman, Harry S. 1949. "Inaugural Address." *The American Presidency Project.* January 20. Accessed November 10, 2020. https://www.presidency.ucsb.edu/documents/inaugural-address-4#axzz1yF36D3DJ.

Trump, Donald. 2020. "Trade & Foreign Policy." *Trump Pence Official Web Site.* Accessed November 24, 2020. https://www.promiseskept.com/achievement/overview/foreign-policy/.

Tucker, Vincent. 1999. "The Myth of Development: A Critique of Euroscentric Discourse." In *Critical Development Theory: Contributions to a New Paradigm,* edited by Ronaldo Munck and Denis O'Hearn, 1–27. London and New York: Zed Books.

Turner, Rachel S. 2007. "The 'Rebirth of Liberalism': The Origins of Neo-Liberal Ideology." *Journal of Political Ideologies* 12 (1): 67–83.

United Conference on Trade and Development. 2001. "World Investment Report 2001." *UNCTAD.* Accessed June 5, 2020. https://unctad.org/en/Docs/wir2001_en.pdf.

———. 2011. "World Investment Report 2011." *UNCTAD.* Accessed June 5, 2020. https://unctad.org/en/PublicationsLibrary/wir2011_en.pdf.

———. 2016. "World Investment Report 2016." *UNCTAD*. Accessed June 5, 2020. https://unctad.org/en/PublicationsLibrary/wir2016_en.pdf.

United Nations Commission on International Trade Law. 2019. "Report of Working Group III (Investor-State Dispute Settlement Reform) on the Work of Its Thirty-Eighth Session (Vienna, 14–18 October 2019)." *The United Nations*. October 23. Accessed October 6, 2020. https://undocs.org/en/A/CN.9/1004.

———. 2020. "The United Nations." *Possible Reform of Investor-State Dispute Settlement (ISDS) Multilateral Instrument on ISDS Reform*. January 16. Accessed October 6, 2020. https://undocs.org/en/A/CN.9/WG.III/WP.194.

United Nations Conference on Trade and Development. 1999. "World Investment Report: Foreign Direct Investment and Development." Accessed May 12, 2020. https://unctad.org/en/Docs/wir1999_en.pdf.

———. 2006. "World Investment Report 2006." *UNCTAD*. Accessed June 5, 2020. https://unctad.org/en/Docs/wir2006_en.pdf.

———. 2007. *Bilateral Investment Treaties in the 1995–2006: Trends in Investment Rule Making*. New York and Geneva.

———. 2020a. *Investment Policy Hub*. Accessed June 6, 2020. https://investmentpolicy.unctad.org/investment-dispute-settlement?status=1000.

———. 2020b. "UNCTAD." *World Investment Report 2019*. Accessed June 5, 2020. https://unctad.org/en/PublicationsLibrary/wir2020_en.pdf.

United Nations Conference on Trade and Employment. 1948. "Final Act and Related Documents." *WTO*. April. Accessed June 28, 2020. (April 1948) UN Doc E/Conf. 2/78. https://www.wto.org/english/docs_e/legal_e/havana_e.pdf.

United Nations, Department of Economic Affairs. 1951. "Measures for the Economic Development of Underdeveloped Countries." *United Nations Digital Library*. May. Accessed June 2, 2020. https://digitallibrary.un.org/record/708544?ln=en.

United Nations Development Programme. 1999. *Human Development Report 1999*. Accessed June 5, 2020. http://hdr.undp.org/sites/default/files/reports/260/hdr_1999_en_nostats.pdf.

Urueña, Rene. 2012. *No Citizens Here: Global Subjects and Participation in International Law*. Brill: Nijhoff.

U.S. Department of Justice. 2011. "Foreign Claims Settlement Commission of the United States: 2011 Annual Report." Accessed June 30, 2020. https://www.justice.gov/sites/default/files/fcsc/docs/annrep11.pdf.

Vandevelde, Kenneth J. 2005. "A Brief History if International Investment Agreements." *U.C. Davis Journal of International Law & Policy* 12 (1): 157–194.

Venezuela Holdings, B.V., et al (case formerly known as Mobil Corporation, Venezuela Holdings, B.V., et al.) v. Bolivarian Republic of Venezuela. 2014. ARB/07/27 (ICSID, October 9).

Vienna Convention on the Law of Treaties. 1969. *Vienna Convention on the Law of Treaties*. Vienna: United Nations, May 23.

Violence Prevention Alliance. n.d. *World Health Organization*. Accessed June 3, 2020. https://www.who.int/violenceprevention/approach/definition/en/.

Wallace, Don, Jr. 1985. "Reviewed Work: International Financial Law by Robert S. Rendell." *The American Journal of International Law* 79 (3): 822.

Wallerstein, Immanuel. 1993. "The Geoculture of Development or the Transformation of Our Geoculture?" *Asian Perspective* 17 (2): 211.
———. 2007. *World System Analysis.* Durham and London: Duke University Press.
———. 2011. *Historical Capitalism with Capitalist Civilization.* London: Verso.
Weissman, Robert. 2017. "Trump's Corporate Cabinet." *HuffPost.* January 10. Accessed November 24, 2020. https://www.huffpost.com/entry/trumps-corporate-cabinet_b_14087282.
Willard, Rainbow, and Sarah Morreau. 2015. "The Canadian Model BIT—A Step in the Right Direction for Canadian Investment in Africa?" *Kluwer Arbitration Blog.* July 18. Accessed October 16, 2020. http://arbitrationblog.kluwerarbitration.com/2015/07/18/the-canadian-model-bit-a-step-in-the-right-direction-for-canadian-investment-in-africa/.
Wolfgang, Marvin E. 1976. "Family Violence and Criminal Behaviour." *Bulletin of the American Academy of Psychiatry and Law* 4 (4): 316.
Wong, Loong. 2009. "The Crisis: A Return to Political Economy?" *Critical Perspectives on International Business* 5: 56–77.
Wood, Dan. 2016. "Imbrications of Coloniaity." In *Resistance and Decolonization*, edited by Amical Cabral, 43–70. Lanham, MD: Rowman & Littlefield.
Wouters, Jan, Duquet Sanderijn, and Nicolas Hachez. 2013. "International Investment Law: The Perpetual Search for Consensus." In *Foreign Direct Investment and Human Development: The Law and Economics of International Investment Agreements*, edited by Oliver de Schuteer, Johan Swinnen, and Jan Wouters, 25–69. London and New York: Routledge.
Wouters, Jan, Sanderijn Duquet, and Nicolas Hachez. 2013. "International Investment Law: The Perpetual Search for Consensus." In *Foreign Direct Investment and Human Development: The Law and Economics of International Agreements*, edited by Oliver de Schuteer, Johan Swinnen, and Jan Wouters, 28. London and New York: Routledge.
Yannaca-Small, Catherine, and Lahra Liberti. 2008. "Definition of Investor and Investment in International Investment Agreements." *International Investment Law: Understanding Concepts and Tracking Innovations.* Accessed June 27, 2020. https://www.oecd.org/investment/internationalinvestmentagreements/internationalinvestmentlawunderstandingconceptsandtrackinginnovations.htm.
Zarra, Giovanni. 2018. "The Issue of Incoherence in Investment Arbitration: Is There Need for a Systemic Reform?" *Chinese Journal of International Law* (17): 137–185.
Zeitler, Helge Elisabeth. 2010. "Full Protection and Security." In *International Investment Law and Comparative Public Law*, edited by Stephan W. Schill, 183–190. Oxford: Oxford University Press.
Zizek, Slavoj. 2009. *Violence.* London: Profile Books.
———. 2011. *Living in the End Times.* London: Verso.

Index

Africa, 2n1, 12, 123
Agosin, Manuel and others, 45
Albania, 22
Allende, Salvador, 91
Americas, the, 1–2, 91, 125
Arendt, Hannah, 16, 23
Argentina, 22, 29, 55, 62, 71–72, 93, 95, 104
Aron, Raymond, 88
Asia, 12
Atlantic Charter, 18
Australia, 21, 30n4, 77, 125
autopoiesis, 13, 99, 109–10

Belgium, 21, 54
Beltran, Lucas, 91
Benjamin, Walter, 10
Bernal, Camila, viii
Bhasin & Manocha, 44
Bilateral Investment Treaty (BIT), 4–5, 12, 19–20, 26, 32, 43–44, 48, 52–54, 59–60, 63, 76, 96, 100, 103, 105–6, 113, 125
Blundel, John, 93
Böhm, Franz, 89
Bolivia, 22, 96, 98
Brazil, 21, 123
Brennan & Ruane, 45
bricoleur, 8n7

Broches, Aron, 4
Brown, Wendy, 97
Buhan, Hussein A., 1, 17, 25–26, 33

Cabral, Amílcar, 16, 78, 112
Calvo, Carlos, 91
Cameron, David, 94
Canada, 11, 12, 21–22, 30, 62, 77, 80, 96, 106, 108
capitalism, 1–2, 4, 9, 15, 25, 35–38, 79, 84–87, 112, 120, 124, 126
capitalists, 2–3, 35, 37–38, 40, 48, 126–28
Caribbean Philosophical Association (CPA), vii, 10
Casey, William, 93
Castro Albarrán, Aniceto, 91
Castro-Gómez, Santiago, 7
centre and centrism, 2, 3, 7, 29–30, 36, 40, 46
Céspedes-Baez, Lina M., viii
Chicago School, 90–91, 94
Chile, 16, 22, 83, 91–93, 109
China, 21, 47, 51, 93, 117
Christian theology, 90
Christie, George, 3, 57, 60
Civil war, 31, 39, 72
coercion, 23–24, 29, 56
Colen, Liseth, 37

Colen, Maertens y Swinnen, 39, 42–43
Colen & Guariso, 46, 60
collective fantasies, 11
collective imagination, 122
collective interests, 109
colonialism, 1, 15–16, 35–36, 56, 96, 101, 118, 120–21
coloniality, 9, 12
colonisation, 1, 32, 41, 52
Columbia Centre on Sustainable Investment, 44
Compañía del Desarrollo de Santa Elena S.A. v Republic of Costa Rica, 59
Comprehensive and Economic Trade Agreement (CETA), 11, 96–97, 108
Congo, 16
Cornel, Drucilla, 64
Coronil, Fernando, 30
Costa Rica, 59, 102
COVID-19, 29, 118
creolisation, 78
creolisation of knowledge, 78
critical theory, 9, 11, 89

D'Amato, Anthony, 109
Davies et al, 38
decolonisation, 4, 19, 25, 39, 52, 57, 63, 115, 119–20
Denmark, 21, 54, 123
Derrida, Jacques, 67
development, 5, 9, 15–17, 19–25, 29, 32, 35–44, 47–48, 51, 53, 60, 94, 115–17, 120–23, 128
Díaz, Juan, viii, 80
disciplinary decadence, 8, 112
Dolzer y Stewvens, 4, 43, 60
Draft Convention on the Protection of Foreign Property, 4, 58
Dussel, Enrique, 1, 6, 9–10, 19, 37, 56, 126
Dutch East India Company, 23

East India Company, 23
Economic Agreement of Bogotá, 55

economics, 3, 5, 26, 36, 38, 47, 90, 97, 126
economy/economies, 2, 5, 7, 12, 16, 18, 20–21, 35, 38, 41–47, 71, 84, 88–89, 91, 97, 122, 125
Egger y Merlo, 44
Egypt, 22
employment, 43, 45, 55
encryption, 8, 12, 20, 33, 59, 65–71, 75, 79–81, 84, 101, 103, 119
Engels, Frederic, 85
environment, the, 6, 17, 20, 26, 63, 111–19
environmental law, 109
environmental protection, 20, 33, 98, 102
environmental rights, 7, 38, 59
epistemic openness, 9
epistemic segregation, 67
epistemic supremacy, 6, 13, 33, 52, 63, 86, 119
epistemic violence, 118
epistemology (Western), 78, 119
epistemologies of ignorance, 67–68
Epstein, Richard, 56
Eslava, Luis, vii
Eurken, Walter, 89
Eurocentrism, 30
European Union (EU), 5, 11, 43, 105

Fanon, Frantz, 2, 5, 9–10, 15, 17, 23, 25–26, 30, 35, 40, 43–44, 51, 69, 78, 122, 127
Fisher, Anthony, 93
Forero, Paola, viii
Forero Ramirez, Juan Carlos, viii
Foucault, Michel, 9n8, 10, 31, 61, 67n2, 75–76, 89, 117
France, 2, 4, 21–22, 54, 77, 89
Franck, Susan, 22, 70, 77, 87
Frankfurt School, 88–89
freedom, 6, 56, 89–90, 92
French Revolution, 31, 94
Freud, Sigmund, 66

Friedman, Milton, 88, 90
Friendship Commerce and Navigation (FCN), 3, 54, 60, 119

Gaitán, Jose Alberto, viii
Garavito, Camilo, viii
García, Laura Victoria, viii
Gerber, David, 89–90
Germany, 4, 21, 30, 52, 77, 88–89, 91–92
globalcentrism, 29–31
global disparity, 17
Global foreign direct investment (FDI), 12, 19–21, 32, 35–39, 41–48, 51, 53, 115–16, 121–22, 128
global governance, 23, 100
Global Institute at Warwick University, vii
globalisation, 5, 10–11, 66, 97, 120, 125
Global Law, 10
global market, 1–6, 12, 18, 19, 25, 30–31, 35, 37–39, 46–49, 51, 115, 123
Global South, 7, 30–31, 104
Göçer, Mercan and Peker, 45
Goodrich, Peter, 67–69, 76, 79, 81
Gordon, Jane Anna, 10, 11
Gordon, Lewis R., vii, 8–10, 25–26, 78, 112, 127
Guardiola-Rivera, Oscar, vii, 1–2, 7, 13, 16, 46, 90, 91, 126
Guzman and Simmons, 96

Hallward-Driemeier, 44
Harms & Méon, 39
Harten, Gus Van, vii, 7, 61–62, 80, 100–102, 105, 109
Hayek, F. A., 56, 88, 91–93
hegemony, 83
historical materialism, 9–10, 127
Hobbes, Thomas, 41
Hong Kong, 21
human rights, 7, 20, 31, 59, 63, 80–81, 98, 102, 104, 109, 111–13, 117, 119

India, 2–3, 21, 23, 45, 107, 113–14, 128
Indigenous Peoples, 96
Indonesia, 21, 32, 62, 63
industrialisation, 11, 39–40, 126; non-, 12, 17, 19, 28, 30, 33, 36
industrial revolution, 3
injustice, 7
Institute for Global Law and Policy (IGLP), vii, 10
International Court of Justice (ICJ), 54, 61, 63, 81
International Economic Law, 9–11, 30
International Financial Institutions, 122–23
International Financial Law (IFL), 36
International Investment (IIL), vii, viii, 1, 4–7, 9–11, 15, 19, 23–31, 33, 36, 41, 47–52, 54–60, 65–71, 74–84, 87, 94–101, 103–13, 115–23, 125, 127–28
International Investment Agreement (IIA), 5, 10, 16, 19, 20, 23–24, 29–30, 36, 39, 51–56, 60–61, 63, 65, 68–70, 80, 82, 84, 95, 101–4, 107–8, 113, 115–19, 122, 124
International Monetary Fund (IMF), 5, 93–94, 121–23
Investment Stat Dispute Settlement (ISDS), 6–7, 12, 21–22, 51, 55, 59, 84, 95, 99–101, 104–8, 111, 113, 118
Ireland, 21
Islamic Republic of Pakistan, 4, 74
Italy, 21–22, 77, 92

Jacobson, Arthur, 99, 109–10
Japan, 21
jobs, 39, 45
Jude, 45
judges, 58, 60, 106, 116
jurisprudence, 61, 70, 103

Kaufman-Kohler, Gabrielle, 77
Kaushal, Asha, 4
Keynesianism, 89–92

Kircheimer, Otto, 89
Koram, Kojo, viii, 67
Korea, the Republic of, 21

Lamm, Carolyn, 77
Langford, Malcolm, Daniel Behn, and Runar Hilleren Lie, 61, 76–78, 105–6
Latin America, 2–3, 12, 45, 93–96, 98, 100
lawyers, 61, 99
Lejour and Salfi, 44
Levine, Eugenia, 61
Linden, Harry Van Der, 28
Lipmann, Walter, 88
Locke, John, 56–57
London (UK), vii, 93

MacLean, Robert Joseph Blaise, vii
Madlingozi, Tshepo, viii
Marcuse, Herbert, 53, 88–89
Marx, Karl, 2n2, 93
McDaid, Paddy, viii
Mendieta, Eduardo, 67, 75
Mexican War, 60
Mexico, 21–22, 102
Mignolo, Walter, 82
Morocco, 22
Morrissey & Udomkerdmongkol, 45
Mulqueen, Tara, viii
Multinational Corporations (MNC), 5, 7, 17, 19, 29–32, 39–40, 48, 59, 63, 87, 102, 115, 117, 123–28

nationalism, 107, 123
nature, 41
Nazi government, 88–89
neoliberalism, 9, 13, 37, 43, 52, 79, 83–84, 87–88, 90, 92, 94, 97–99, 117, 122
Netherlands, The, 4, 21–22, 75, 77
Neumann, Franz, 53, 88–89
Neumayer and Spess, 44
Newman, Graeme, 24
New York City, 93
New Zealand, 77

Nicaragua, 16
Nkrumah, Kwame, 16, 18

Obama, Barack, 106
Olarte, Carolina, viii
oppression, 26, 78
Organisation for Economic Co-operation and Development (OECD), 4, 22, 54–55, 57–58

Paraguay, 22
Paris, 70, 88, 91
Paris, Rodrigo, viii
Patterson, William, 2n4
Pecheux, Michel, 67, 79, 86
Peck, Jamie, 83–84, 88–94, 97, 98
Peck and Tickell, 84, 94, 97–98
Performance Based Allocation (PBA), 94
Perry-Kessaris, Amanda, 3, 10, 19–20, 43, 45, 80
Peru, 5n5, 11, 22, 43, 93
Philippines, 22
politics, 3, 26, 40, 81, 83, 97, 120; bio-, 89
Pollock, Friedrich, 89
Pontón Serra, Juan Pablo, vii
Portugal, 123
Post-colonial bilateralism, 4
poverty, 11, 41, 43
Prieto-Rios, Enrique, 61, 67, 80, 83, 88, 96, 101, 107, 121
privatisation, 45, 71, 94, 97–98
property, 3–4, 23, 54, 59–60, 63, 74, 84, 88, 92, 94, 97; foreign, 51, 53; intellectual, 42, 46, 125; private, 48, 52, 56–57, 89, 93, 95, 98
Pulido, Ivan, viii

Quijano, Anibal, 120

racism, 63, 118
Rahimi, Sadeq, 66–67
Reagan, Ronald, 4
Restrepo Abondano, Jose Manuel, viii

Rivas, Daniel, 61
Roberts, Anthea, 6–7, 69
Roesel Juan José, viii
Romania, 22, 60
Röpke, Wilhelm, 88
Rottleuthner, Hubert, 8, 13, 99
Rueff, Jacques, 88
Ruiz-Wilkey, Jenny, viii
Russia, 21–22, 60
Rüstow, Alexander, 88

Salacuse and Sullivan, 44
Sánchez Lissen, Rocio, 91
Sanin-Restrepo, Ricardo, 66, 68–69, 81
Sardá, Juan, 91
Saudia Arabia, 21
Sauvy, Alfred, 12
Schill, Stephan W, 7, 55–56, 100–101, 103–4
Schneiderman, David, 10–11, 71
Schwartz, Pedro, 91
Sharma, Kanika, viii
Shaw, George Bernard, 93n4
socialism, 15, 25, 91, 93
Sornajah, M., 98
Sousa Santos, Boaventura de, 84, 97
South Africa, 2n1, 10, 123
South America, 32, 114–24
sovereignty, 3–4, 43, 63
Spain, 2, 21–22, 54, 74–75, 77, 91–92
Sri Lanka, 22
Subhashini, Alí, 19
Suresh, Mayur, viii
Sweden, 4, 21, 77
Switzerland, 21, 74, 77

Tan and Faundez, 5, 11, 16, 23, 30, 95
Tataryn, Anastasia, viii
taxes, 29, 38, 46, 79
telecommunications, 38
Third World, 8, 11–12, 16–20, 25, 32–33, 35, 37–40, 43–48, 52, 54, 64n5, 78, 88, 116, 121, 124, 127–28
Tienhaara, K., 62
totalitarianism, 91

Truman, Harry S., 40
Turkey, 21–22, 93
Turner, Rachel, 88, 91–92, 95

Ukraine, 22, 72–73, 104
underdevelopment, 40–41
United Arab Emirates, 21
United Kingdom, 2, 4, 77, 92–93, 104, 123–24
United Nations (UN), 5n6, 20–22, 36–38, 40, 42–44, 55, 70, 101, 104, 106; Conference on Trade and Development, 19
United Nations Commission on International Trade (UNCITRAL), 73, 100, 104–6, 113
United States Department of Justice, 60
United States Department of State, 107
Universidad del Rosario, viii

Valued Added Tax (VAT), 73
Vásquez de Mella, Juan, 91
Venezuela, 22, 35, 62, 74, 96, 100
violence (systematic), 8–9, 12, 15–17, 21–35, 51, 64, 66, 81, 83–84, 99–100, 115, 118, 120–21, 127–28

Wall, Illan, vii
Wall Street, 93
Wayenberge, Elisa Van, 93
wealth, 26, 36, 67, 121, 123, 126, 128; public, 57
Webb, Beatrice and Sidney, 93
William III, 2n4
Williamson, John, 93
Wolfgang, Marvin E., 24
World Bank, 4–5, 22, 38, 43, 45, 58, 93–94, 121–23
World Trade Organization (WTO), 61, 63, 81, 109, 125
World Wars, 18, 52, 89

Zarra, Giovanni, 100–101, 103, 105
Žižek, Slavoj, 9, 16–18, 24–25, 27–29, 81, 85–86

About the Author

Enrique Prieto-Rios is currently Director of the Research Group of International Law, Research Director and Associate Professor at the Faculty of Law – Universidad del Rosario. Enrique holds a Phd in Law from Birkbeck – University of London, MA in International Law The London College UCK and Attorney at Law – Universidad del Rosario Bogotá. Enrique's research focuses on International Economic Law, International Investment Law and Business and Human Rights. Enrique is Commissioner at the Advisory Commission on Peace and Human Rights that was created by the 2016 Peace Accord. Enrique has been a visiting lecturer at the School of Law—Universidad de los Andes, a visiting fellow at Osgoode the School of Law – University of York, a visiting fellow at the School of Law – University of Warwick and a sessional lecturer at the School of Law – Birkbeck University of London. Enrique has been the Director of the British and Colombian Lawyers Association—BRICOL, intern at the International Bar Association—IBA—and a consultant for law firms in Bogotá and in London.

www.ingramcontent.com/pod-product-compliance
Lightning Source LLC
Chambersburg PA
CBHW020124010526
44115CB00008B/967